# Success
## Assessment Papers

# KS3 English

LEVELS
6-7

Cherie S. Rowe

level showing
attainment target

paper number for
quick reference

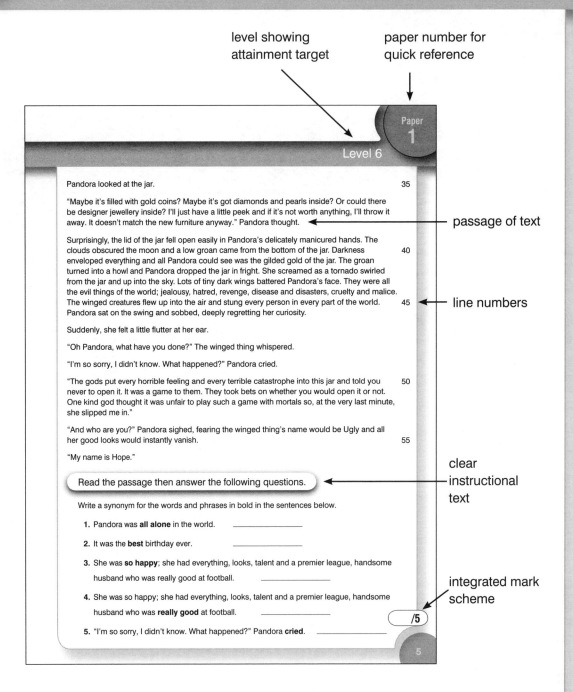

Paper
**1**

Level 6

Pandora looked at the jar.                                                                                    35

"Maybe it's filled with gold coins? Maybe it's got diamonds and pearls inside? Or could there
be designer jewellery inside? I'll just have a little peek and if it's not worth anything, I'll throw it
away. It doesn't match the new furniture anyway." Pandora thought. ◄──── passage of text

Surprisingly, the lid of the jar fell open easily in Pandora's delicately manicured hands. The
clouds obscured the moon and a low groan came from the bottom of the jar. Darkness            40
enveloped everything and all Pandora could see was the gilded gold of the jar. The groan
turned into a howl and Pandora dropped the jar in fright. She screamed as a tornado swirled
from the jar and up into the sky. Lots of tiny dark wings battered Pandora's face. They were all
the evil things of the world; jealousy, hatred, revenge, disease and disasters, cruelty and malice.
The winged creatures flew up into the air and stung every person in every part of the world.   45   ◄── line numbers
Pandora sat on the swing and sobbed, deeply regretting her curiosity.

Suddenly, she felt a little flutter at her ear.

"Oh Pandora, what have you done?" The winged thing whispered.

"I'm so sorry, I didn't know. What happened?" Pandora cried.

"The gods put every horrible feeling and every terrible catastrophe into this jar and told you     50
never to open it. It was a game to them. They took bets on whether you would open it or not.
One kind god thought it was unfair to play such a game with mortals so, at the very last minute,
she slipped me in."

"And who are you?" Pandora sighed, fearing the winged thing's name would be Ugly and all
her good looks would instantly vanish.                                                                  55

"My name is Hope."

> Read the passage then answer the following questions. ◄──── clear
> instructional
> text

Write a synonym for the words and phrases in bold in the sentences below.

1. Pandora was **all alone** in the world.          _____

2. It was the **best** birthday ever.          _____

3. She was **so happy**; she had everything, looks, talent and a premier league, handsome
   husband who was really good at football.          _____

4. She was so happy; she had everything, looks, talent and a premier league, handsome    integrated mark
   husband who was **really good** at football.          _____                scheme

5. "I'm so sorry, I didn't know. What happened?" Pandora **cried**.          _____

   /5

5

# Contents

| PAPER 1 | 4 |
| PAPER 2 | 12 |
| PAPER 3 | 18 |
| PAPER 4 | 24 |
| PAPER 5 | 31 |
| PAPER 6 | 38 |
| PAPER 7 | 44 |
| PAPER 8 | 51 |
| PAPER 9 | 58 |
| PAPER 10 | 64 |
| Glossary | 71 |
| Progress grid | 72 |
| Answer booklet | 1–8 |

## PAPER 1

### 'Pandora's Gift'

Pandora was all alone in the world. She didn't really have a father or a mother. Zeus, the god of all gods, told Hephaestus, the god of sculptures, to make the most beautiful girl in the world, so he made Pandora. He never told anyone why he told Hephaestus to make the most beautiful girl in the world. The truth was Zeus was angry. He was angry because Prometheus, a Titan, had stolen his fire and given it to the mortals. He thought sending the most beautiful girl in   5 the world to earth with a terrible gift would be a good way to punish the mortals. In fact, her name, Pandora, meant gift in Greek. On Pandora's day of birth, each god gave her a gift. It was the best birthday ever. Venus, the god of love, gave her the gift of beauty. Hermes, the god of persuasion, gave her the powerful gift of the gab; she could convince anyone of anything! The god Apollo gave her the gift of music; she could play any instrument ever invented and sing like  10 a lark. She was sure to be signed by a leading record label. The last gift was the one from Zeus. It was a beautiful, ornate gilded gold jar. The lid was tightly screwed down and the gods told her never ever to open it, but to keep the jar with her at all times.

Epimetheus, a striking, floppy-haired youth, fell in love with Pandora. He asked his brother, Prometheus, whether he knew her.  15

"Pandora? The gift of the gods? You can't like her surely!" Prometheus scoffed.

"But brother, when she smiles, the sun shines. When she laughs, the birds sing. How could any man not fall in love with her?" Epimetheus replied dreamily.

"Stay away from her. She's nothing but trouble. If the gods have given her gifts, then beware. Any girl worth her salt works to get where she is."  20

"I'm not interested in your independent women, Prometheus. They all have too much to say for themselves." Epimetheus retorted haughtily.

"Don't say I didn't warn you!" Prometheus cautioned.

Epimetheus ignored his brother's warning and proposed to Pandora on bended knee under a weeping willow by the river.  25

On the evening of their wedding day, after all the feasting, drinking and dancing, Pandora was exhausted. She had spent all day thanking everyone for coming, looking pretty and sipping champagne. She had even sung her heart out to all the number ones and beat everyone on SongSuperStar. Kissing Epimetheus, ignoring the dark looks of his brother Prometheus, she picked up her gold gilded jar and went out to the garden to the swing. She slipped off her  30 stilettos and the cool grass eased her aching feet. She clung to the jar as she swung gently under the moonlight. The moonlight reflected the gilded gold of the jar and dazzled Pandora. She was so happy; she had everything, looks, talent and a premier league, handsome husband who was really good at football.

Pandora looked at the jar.                                                                                              35

"Maybe it's filled with gold coins? Maybe it's got diamonds and pearls inside? Or could there be designer jewellery inside? I'll just have a little peek and if it's not worth anything, I'll throw it away. It doesn't match the new furniture anyway." Pandora thought.

Surprisingly, the lid of the jar fell open easily in Pandora's delicately manicured hands. The clouds obscured the moon and a low groan came from the bottom of the jar. Darkness            40
enveloped everything and all Pandora could see was the gilded gold of the jar. The groan turned into a howl and Pandora dropped the jar in fright. She screamed as a tornado swirled from the jar and up into the sky. Lots of tiny dark wings battered Pandora's face. They were all the evil things of the world; jealousy, hatred, revenge, disease and disasters, cruelty and malice. The winged creatures flew up into the air and stung every person in every part of the world.            45
Pandora sat on the swing and sobbed, deeply regretting her curiosity.

Suddenly, she felt a little flutter at her ear.

"Oh Pandora, what have you done?" The winged thing whispered.

"I'm so sorry, I didn't know. What happened?" Pandora cried.

"The gods put every horrible feeling and every terrible catastrophe into this jar and told you            50
never to open it. It was a game to them. They took bets on whether you would open it or not. One kind god thought it was unfair to play such a game with mortals so, at the very last minute, she slipped me in."

"And who are you?" Pandora sighed, fearing the winged thing's name would be Ugly and all her good looks would instantly vanish.                                                                                                  55

"My name is Hope."

## Read the passage then answer the following questions.

Write a synonym for the words and phrases in bold in the sentences below.

1. Pandora was **all alone** in the world.          _____

2. It was the **best** birthday ever.          _____

3. She was **so happy**; she had everything, looks, talent and a premier league, handsome husband who was really good at football.          _____

4. She was so happy; she had everything, looks, talent and a premier league, handsome husband who was **really good** at football.          _____

5. "I'm so sorry, I didn't know. What happened?" Pandora **cried**.          _____

/5

Draw lines to match the words in bold to their definitions in the right-hand column.

6. 'Hermes, the god of **persuasion**, gave her the powerful gift of the gab…'

to respond quickly in an insulting or sharp way

7. 'The last gift was the one from Zeus. It was a beautiful, **ornate** gilded gold jar.'

the wish to do harm or cause pain to someone

8. '"I'm not interested in your independent women, Prometheus. They all have too much to say for themselves." Epimetheus **retorted** haughtily.'

to convince somebody to do something

9. '"I'm not interested in your independent women, Prometheus. They all have too much to say for themselves." Epimetheus retorted **haughtily**.'

lots of detailed decoration

10. 'Lots of tiny dark wings battered Pandora's face. They were all the evil things of the world; jealousy, hatred, revenge, diseases and disasters, cruelty and **malice**.'

to behave in a self-important way

/5

Underline the subordinate clause or clauses in the following sentences.

11. Zeus, the god of all gods, told Hephaestus to make the most beautiful girl in the world.

12. Zeus ordered Hephaestus, the god of sculptures, to make the most beautiful girl in the world.

13. Venus, the god of love, gave her the gift of beauty.

14. Hermes, the god of persuasion, gave her the powerful gift of the gab.

15. The god Apollo gave her the gift of music, she could play any instrument ever invented.

16. Pandora sat on the swing and sobbed, deeply regretting her curiosity.

/6

Rewrite the following simple sentences as **complex sentences** without using the connectives *and*, *but*, *as*, or *so*.

**17.** The guests danced. They cheered the happy couple. They threw confetti.

_____

_____

**18.** The sun radiated bliss. The morning of the wedding day arrived. Pandora was excited.

_____

_____

**19.** Pandora was scared. She shivered. She ran inside.

_____

_____

**20.** Epimetheus soothed her. He spoke calmly to her. He held her hand.

_____

_____

**21.** Hope fluttered past Pandora. Pandora looked up. She smiled faintly.

_____

_____

/5

Fill the gaps in this summary of the story.

**22–31.** The main character in the story is _____. She was made by the god of

_____ to be the most _____ girl in the world. She received

many gifts from the gods, _____, _____, _____

and _____ which she must never open. _____ warned his

brother _____ to be cautious of girls bearing gifts from the gods, but to

no avail. _____ proposed to Pandora who accepted.

/10

List three similarities between the first paragraph and last paragraph of the story.

32. _____

33. _____

34. _____

/3

Answer these questions.

35. What is the effect of the short, opening sentence of the story?

_____

36. Why was Pandora all alone in the world at the beginning of the story?

_____

/2

What expectations does the writer create before Pandora opens the jar? List three expectations and find a quotation to support each one.

| Expectation | Quotation |
|---|---|
| 37. | 38. |
| 39. | 40. |
| 41. | 42. |

/6

Identify three areas of conflict in the story and find a quotation for each one.

| Conflict | Quotation |
|---|---|
| 43. | 44. |
| 45. | 46. |
| 47. | 48. |

/6

Answer these questions.

**49.** What event creates complication in the story?

_____

_____

**50.** What unattractive feature does the writer give Pandora?

_____

_____

**51.** Find a quotation to show where the writer changes the mood of the story.

_____

_____

/3

Choose three 'images' from the text to show how the writer contrasts the mood of the story.

| Cheerful mood | Sombre mood |
|---|---|
| 52. | 53. |
| 54. | 55. |
| 56. | 57. |

/6

Find five quotations from the passage that show the writer has modernised the story.

58. _____

59. _____

60. _____

61. _____

62. _____

/5

Answer these questions.

63. Why do you think the writer has included contemporary references in a myth?

_____

_____

64. What does the following quotation suggest about Pandora's character?

'"I'll just have a little peek and if it's not worth anything, I'll throw it away. It doesn't match the new furniture anyway." Pandora thought.'

_____

_____

**65.** Select another quotation to provide extra support to your answer to question 64.

_____

_____

**66.** Which point of view is the story written from?

_____

_____

**67.** Why does the writer use the word 'every' in 'The winged creatures flew up into the air and stung every person in every part of the world' and 'The gods put every horrible feeling and every terrible catastrophe into this jar and told you never to open it'?

_____

_____

**68.** Explain why Hope was put into the jar.

_____

_____

**69.** Why is the meaning of Pandora's name, 'gift of the gods', **ironic**?

_____

_____

**70.** Explain the meaning of the title of the story.

_____

_____

/8

/70

## PAPER 2

### 'Miss Blake's Cover Lesson'

| | |
|---|---:|
| The classroom was irregular: | |
| Dusty perfume bottles | |
| Boxes of beads, threads, wires. | |
| "Stuff to inspire" she supposed. | |
| No register, no date, no objectives on the board | 5 |
| She tut-tutted and wrote up her name, underlined it, twice. | |
| Miss Blake. Cover Teacher. | |
| Now they would know who to ask for help. | |
| | |
| Pupils poured in eagerly; got themselves ready | |
| Found art materials with ease. | 10 |
| Brushing on blue wash imitating Gaudi | |
| Colouring in between the lines. | |
| Some girls whisper, some sit alone | |
| Some sit in paired armoury. | |
| Pop, hip hop and bass buzzing from earphones | 15 |
| Miss Blake suspected, in Art, this was allowed. | |
| | |
| She walked between them | |
| Not knowing their names. | |
| Envious of their confidence | |
| Knowing the difference | 20 |
| Between pastels and blocks | |
| How to mix up PVA | |
| How to stitch the border of Rousseau | |
| How easily inspiration came to them. | |
| | |
| No one asked her a question | 25 |
| No one put up their hand | |
| They only looked surprised, faintly amused | |
| At her efforts at doodling, | |
| She was never taught the ways of seeing in Maths | |
| She screwed up her paper | 30 |
| She started on some sums | |
| And wished for the vividness of their imagination. | |

Read the poem then answer the following questions.

Underline the correct word to complete each sentence.

1. The poem is written from the (first / second / third) person point of view.

2. This point of view means that the poem is (subjective / objective).

/2

Answer these questions.

3. Who is the main character in the poem? _____

4. Why is Miss Blake taking an art class? _____

5. What subject does Miss Blake usually teach? _____

6. Which line gives you evidence of this? _____

7. Do you think Miss Blake prefers a tidy or an untidy classroom? _____

8. Which line from the poem supports your answer to question 7? _____

9. Why do you think Miss Blake underlines her name twice on the board?

_____

10. Does the poem suggest that Miss Blake wants the pupils to ask her for help? _____

/8

What impression does the poet give of the art pupils? Draw lines to match the statements with the textual quotations.

| | |
|---|---|
| 11. lines 19–23 | The pupils are confident in their art skills |
| 12. lines 19 and 24 | The classroom is a stimulating environment |
| 13. lines 25–26 | The pupils settle down to their work quickly |
| 14. line 30 | Miss Blake likes order, discipline and authority in her classroom |
| 15. lines 5–8 | Miss Blake thinks she is not very good at art |
| 16. lines 9–10 | Miss Blake wanted to get involved in the art lesson |
| 17. lines 2–4 | There are different expectations of behaviour in the art class |
| 18. line 16 | Miss Blake feels uncomfortable in this environment because the pupils know more about art than she does |
| 19. line 32 | The pupils do not need Miss Blake for anything |
| 20. line 28 | Miss Blake resented the pupils' creativity |

/10

**21–25.** Choose one of the words or phrases from the box to fill each gap in the sentences below.

| strict | dismissive | subject | tone | cover teacher |

The title of the poem tells us that Miss Blake is a _____. She

is the _____ of the poem. The first line of the poem sets the

_____ of the poem because the experience is going to be

unusual for Miss Blake. The phrases 'Stuff to inspire' and that she 'tut-tutted' suggest

that Miss Blake is _____ of the stimulating environment of the art

class. The first verse also tells us that Miss Blake is quite a _____

teacher who likes to be in charge.

/5

For each of the short extracts below, write the technical term used by the poet.

**26.** 'Brushing on blue wash' _____

**27.** 'Some girls whisper, some sit alone / Some sit in paired armoury' _____

**28.** 'Boxes of beads, threads, wires' _____

**29.** 'No register, no date, no objectives' _____

**30.** 'Pupils poured in' _____

**31.** 'Pop, hip hop' _____

**32.** 'bass buzzing' _____

**33.** 'Envious of their confidence / Knowing the difference' _____

**34.** 'How to mix up PVA / how to stitch the border... / how easily...' _____

**35.** 'some sums' _____

/10

Suggest alternative words for the following words or phrases.

**36.** envious _____

**37.** irregular _____

**38.** point of view _____

**39.** bright _____

**40.** show _____

/5

Unscramble these letters to make a word connected to the poem.

**41.** pin to raisin _____

**42.** ivy tire cat _____

**43.** coo slur _____

**44.** giant aim I on _____

**45.** cut speeds _____

/5

Choose the correct adverb from the box below to add to the following sentences.

| never | first | then | always | before | easily |
|-------|-------|------|--------|--------|--------|

**46.** Miss Blake _____ drew pictures.

**47–48.** _____ the pupils collected their art materials and _____ sat down to work.

**49.** Miss Blake _____ put her name on the board.

**50.** Miss Blake started to doodle _____ screwing up her paper.

**51.** The pupils continued with their art work _____.

/6

Put the essay plan in order by writing the correct paragraph number in the right-hand column.

| Opening sentence | Paragraph number |
|------------------|------------------|
| **52.** The poem ends with Miss Blake trying to get involved in the lesson but failing. | |
| **53.** This contrasts with the pupils who are relaxed in the classroom and enjoy their lesson. | |
| **54.** Miss Blake's reaction to the Art classroom is negative. | |
| **55.** In this verse, the poet emphasises how uncomfortable Miss Blake is in the classroom. | |

/4

Look at the following definitions and insert the correct letters to spell the words.

56. Oven to heat pottery                                              k__ __ n

57. Picture made with lots of different pieces of materials          co__ __ a __e

58. Display with lots of pictures                                    __ __hibit__ __ __

59. Band of decoration running along the wall of a room             fr__ __ z__

60. A particular point of view                                       pers__ __ c__ __ v__

61. A type of paint                                                  ac__ __ li__

/6

Rewrite the following sentences to make them passive.

62. Miss Blake asks the pupils if they need help.

_____

_____

63. Miss Blake finished the art lesson early.

_____

_____

64. Everyone can learn to draw with patience.

_____

_____

65. The school is building a new art and design block.

_____

_____

/4

Explain the effect of the punctuation or lack of punctuation in the following lines from the poem.

66. 'Miss Blake. Cover Teacher.'

_____

_____

_____

**67.** 'Miss Blake suspected, in Art, this was allowed.'

_____

_____

_____

**68.** 'Pupils poured in eagerly; got themselves ready / Found art materials with ease.'

_____

_____

_____

**69.** 'Brushing on blue wash imitating Gaudi / Colouring in between the lines.'

_____

_____

_____

**70.** 'Envious of their confidence
Knowing the difference
Between pastels and blocks
How to mix up PVA
How to stitch the border of Rousseau
How easily inspiration came to them.'

_____

_____

_____

_____

/5

/70

## PAPER 3

**'Twelfth Night, or What You Will'** by William Shakespeare

I. ii, *Enter Viola, a Captain, and sailors*

VIOLA

What country, friends, is this?

CAPTAIN

This is Illyria, lady.

VIOLA

And what should I do in Illyria?

My brother, he is in Elysium[1].

Perchance he is not drowned. What think you sailors?

CAPTAIN

It is perchance that you yourself were saved.

VIOLA

O my poor brother!- and so perchance may he be.

CAPTAIN

True, madam, and to comfort you with chance,

Assure yourself, after our ship did split,

When you and those poor number saved with you

Hung on our driving boat, I saw your brother,

Most provident[2] in peril, bind himself-

Courage and hope both teaching him the practice-

To a strong mast that lived upon the sea,

Where, like Arion[3] on the dolphin's back,

I saw him hold acquaintance with the waves

So long as I could see.

VIOLA *(giving money)*

For saying so, there's gold.

Mine own escape unfoldeth to my hope,

Whereto thy speech serves for authority,

The like of him. Know'st thou this country?

CAPTAIN

Ay, madam, well, for I was bred and born

Not three hours' travel from this very place.

VIOLA

Who governs here?

CAPTAIN

A noble duke, in nature

As in name.

---

[1]A mythological name for the place after death

[2]Preparing for the future

[3]An Ancient Greek poet who wrote a myth about being kidnapped by pirates and rescued by dolphins

VIOLA
What is his name?

CAPTAIN
Orsino.

VIOLA

Orsino. I have heard my father name him.
He was a bachelor then.

CAPTAIN

And so is now, or was so very late,
For but a month ago I went from hence,
And then 'twas fresh in murmur -as, you know,
What great ones do the less will prattle of-
That he did seek the love of fair Olivia.

## Read the extract from the play then answer the following questions.

1. What act and scene is the extract taken from? _____

2. What do you think has happened before the scene starts?

_____

3. Why do you think Shakespeare includes sailors but does not give them any lines?

_____

4. Why are the characters' names in capitals?

_____

5. What stage direction is given in the extract?

_____

/5

## Write a definition of each of the following words by working out the meaning from the context.

6. perchance _____

7. split _____

8. acquaintance _____

9. bachelor _____

10. prattle _____

/5

19

Answer these questions.

**11.** Why do you think Shakespeare makes the first line of the scene the question, 'What country, friends, is this?'

_____

**12.** Who is Viola talking to when she refers to 'friends'?

_____

**13.** Where in the text does Viola show that she thinks her brother is dead? Write the quotation.

_____

**14.** How do you think the sailors respond when Viola asks them what they think?

_____

**15.** Where was the Captain born and bred? _____

**16.** Who was the last person to see Viola's brother? _____

**17.** Who is the ruler of Illyria? _____

**18.** Has Viola met the ruler of Illyria? _____

**19.** What is he like? _____

**20.** Who is Olivia? _____

/10

Rewrite the following lines in modern English.

**21.** 'What country, friends, is this?' _____

**22.** 'What think you sailors?' _____

**23.** 'For saying so, there's gold.' _____

**24.** 'And so is now, or was so very late.' _____

**25.** 'For but a month ago I went from hence' _____

/5

**Answer these questions.**

**26–27.** What two characteristics does the Captain tell Viola that her brother had?

_____

**28.** What was Viola's brother doing when the Captain saw him?

_____

**29.** Where in the text does Viola show that she trusts what the Captain says about her brother?

Write the quotation. _____

**30.** When was the last time the Captain was in Illyria? _____

/5

**Fill in the gaps with your comments or quotations from the text.**

**31–40.** In this scene, the audience is introduced to Viola who has landed on-shore after

being shipwrecked. Her third question, '_____'

tells the audience that even though she has been saved from the storm, she is upset at

being separated from her brother who she believes is in '_____',

which means she thinks he is _____. Shakespeare shows us

that she is upset because she changes her mind quickly in the next line and says

'_____'. However, we know she is not

certain about this because she asks _____ what they think.

The Captain's purpose in this scene is to _____

Viola that her brother has survived the storm. He does this first by reminding Viola that

she has survived; '_____'.

Shakespeare gives the Captain a variety of words to convince Viola such as;

'_____', '_____' and '_____'.

/10

Imagine you are a director helping the actress play Viola. Draw lines to match the actions to the quotations.

41. 'Orsino. I have heard my father name him.'

Kneel and put hands together in prayer

42. 'For saying so, there's gold.'

Get up and walk to the Captain and give him something

43. 'O my poor brother!- and so perchance may he be.'

Run to each sailor and touch their arm or shoulder to get them to answer the question

44. 'What think you sailors?'

Put hands to face and sob silently

45. 'My brother, he is in Elysium.'

Put hands to heart

/5

Draw lines to match the technical term in the right-hand column to the quotations in the left-hand column.

46. 'like Arion on the dolphin's back'

personification

47. 'Whereto thy speech serves for authority, The like of him. Know'st thou this country?'

sibilance

48. 'I saw him hold acquaintance with the waves'

end-rhyme

49. 'Assure yourself, after our ship did split'

alliteration

50. 'A noble duke, in nature / As in name.'

simile

/5

Write true or false for the following expectations about the play.

51. Viola will meet Orsino. _____

52. The opening of a tragedy usually has a hopeful beginning and ends with the death of the main character. _____

**53.** The opening of a comedy usually has a sad beginning and a happy ending.

_____

**54.** Viola and Orsino will fall in love. _____

**55.** Viola's brother is dead. _____

**56.** Viola will probably die in the play. _____

**57.** In Shakespeare's time, only rich people went to the theatre. _____

**58.** Shakespeare's plays contain a mixture of verse and prose. _____

**59.** Shakespeare only wrote comedies. _____

**60.** Shakespeare's plays are still relevant to us today because they deal with human nature, which does not change. _____                   /10

Unscramble each set of letters to make a word related to drama. There is a clue for each anagram.

**61.** A apple us      The audience usually do this at the end of the play. _____

**62.** Why girl tap   The author of the drama. _____

**63.** Sight plot    Actors need to stand in this to be seen. _____

**64.** Rips movies   To make up a drama without a script. _____

**65.** Cut me so     Actors wear this on stage. _____

**66.** Cot rider     The person who tells the actors what to do. _____

**67.** For men pacer This is the presentation of the play. _____

**68.** A rash reel    This is where the actors practise the play. _____

**69.** Can enter     This is where the actors come onto the stage. _____

**70.** Art thee      The building where the play is staged. _____   /10

/70

## PAPER 4

### 'Millennium Development Goal 1 – To eradicate extreme poverty and hunger'

**Target – Between 1990 and 2015, halve the proportion of people whose income is less than $1 a day.**

**Target – Between 1990 and 2015, halve the proportion of people who suffer from hunger.**

In 1990, nearly 28 per cent of people in low- and middle-income countries were living on less than $1 (50p) a day. Many people living at this level of poverty cannot afford to pay for basic                    5
requirements such as food. The aim of the first Millennium Development Goal is to reduce this figure to 14 per cent by 2015, thereby lifting more than 500 million people out of extreme poverty. While this will not signify a complete eradication of poverty, it will bring the world closer to a stage when all its people will have the minimum necessary to feed and clothe themselves.

### Millennium Development Goal 1 – To eradicate extreme poverty and hunger        10

Today 1.2 billion people around the world live on less than $1 a day; while almost 850 million go hungry every night. The greatest number of poor people live in South Asia, but the proportion is highest in sub-Saharan Africa, where over 40 percent of the population continues to live on one dollar a day or less. In fact, the number of poor people in this region has actually increased over the years. The main aim of the first Millennium Development Goal (MDG) is          15
to halve the number of people living in extreme poverty from 1990 levels by 2015. While this will not mean a complete eradication of poverty, it will bring the world closer to a stage where all its people will have at least the minimum necessary to feed and clothe themselves. The proportion of people living in extreme poverty worldwide fell from nearly a third to less than a fifth between 1990 and 2004. If this trend is sustained, the MDG poverty reduction target will          20
be met for the world as a whole and for most regions. However, sub-Saharan Africa is not on track to reach the target. It is vital that the world community works together to reduce poverty and so meet people's basic needs. Much could be achieved by reforming international trade, so that developing countries receive fair prices for their goods. **Halting climate change will also be essential if the progress that has been achieved worldwide is not to be wiped out**   25
**by floods, droughts and food shortages**. In a world in which many people are better off than ever before, it is unacceptable that so many others should be struggling to survive.[4]

### Alpaca farming in Peru

Lucas Riquelme is seven years old and lives in Macusani, a small town high up in the Andes in Peru. His father owns a herd of alpacas, which he farms for their wool. Although Lucas's           30
family is relatively well-off, most alpaca farmers are very poor, earning less than two dollars a day on average, and cannot meet their basic needs. They live in small shacks with no heating and barely enough to eat.

**Macusani is on the side of a mountain called Allinccapac, which is topped by a glacier. The whole of the mountain-top used to be white with snow, but nowadays great                    35
expanses of bare mountain are visible. The glacier is melting away because of climate change. This worries the people very much, because their water supply comes from the melted snow and ice that flow down in the warmer season of the year. Lucas's teacher,**

---

[4] 1 UNDP Annual Report, 2008

Carlos Enriquez, says 'Our students are aware that there is a possible water crisis coming if nothing is done.' Climate change could cause many people to have to leave their homes, abandon their way of life and find another way of supporting themselves. 40

Meeting the MDGs will help lift people like the alpaca farmers of Macusani out of poverty. However, the challenge of climate change also needs to be addressed – rich countries should pay to help poor countries cope with its effects, so that people like those in Macusani will be better able to adapt to the changes that are being forced upon them. 45

**Definitions of poverty**

*Relative poverty*: Measures how far a household's income falls below the average income in a country.

*Absolute poverty*: Measures the number of people living below a certain level or the number of people who cannot afford basic goods and services. 50

50p a day represents a minimum standard of living in the poorest countries, so the 1.2 billion people who today live on less than this are living in absolute poverty.

**In the UK**

• Two million children live in workless households.

• Over one in five people lives in poverty. 55

**In the world**

• 850 million people go to bed hungry every day.

• About 2.6 billion people (nearly half the world's population) live on less than £1.00 a day.

• 1.1 billion people have no clean water.

• 2.6 billion people have no sanitation. 60

• 1.6 billion people (about one-quarter of the world's population) have no electricity.

Sources: United Nations Development Programme, World Bank and New Policy Institute (www.poverty.org.uk)

**Jobs mean food for Ethiopia's poor**

A combination of failed rains and rising prices led to food shortages across Ethiopia in 2008. 65
In eight regions, a Department for International Development (DFID) funded programme ensured that some of Ethiopia's most vulnerable people were able to survive.

The programme operated by providing food and money to at-risk households in exchange for their work improving public facilities. Communities benefit from better roads and water points, and individuals are able to avoid famine by buying food-generating assets like cattle. 70

Aster Kurma lives with her husband and their eight children in the district of Kedida Gamela, about 350 kilometres south of Addis Ababa. The region, which is vulnerable to drought, was badly affected by the low rainfall. Five days a week, Aster works for the programme on soil conservation and tree planting projects, helping to turn the parched land around her home into lush green plots. Payment comes in the form of food or money. As well as meeting 75
Aster's immediate needs by providing her with a stable source of food, the new programme is equipping her for the longer term. She has been able to buy farming tools and cattle, opening up new opportunities for the whole family. "I'm not only able to feed my children, but I can send them to school as well," she says.

Read the passage then answer the following questions.

Fill in the gaps in the sentences below using information from the passage.

1. _____ people in the world live in extreme poverty today.

2. _____% of the world's population have no electricity.

3. By 2015 the MDG has an objective to rescue _____ people from extreme poverty.

4. The MDG will use the levels of extreme poverty in _____ as its starting point.

5. In the United Kingdom, _____ children live with parents or carers who are unemployed.

6. In the United Kingdom, _____ out of _____ people do not live in poverty.

7. The proportion of people living in poverty has increased in _____ over the years.

8. The MDG has an objective to achieve its target by _____.

9. In 14 years, the proportion of people living in extreme poverty fell from
   _____ to _____.

10. Worldwide, _____ people are without sewage collection.

/10

Match the words in the box below to the correct definitions and state which line they appear in.

| asset | eradicate | relative | absolute | proportion |
|-------|-----------|----------|----------|------------|
| reform | vulnerable | sustained | trend | alpaca |

11. South American long-haired animal similar to a llama  _____

12. A general movement, direction  _____

13. To improve something by removing faults  _____

14. To make something long lasting  _____

15. Unquestionable, certain  _____

**16.** At risk from physical or emotional harm     _____

**17.** To get rid of something completely     _____

**18.** Somebody or something that is useful     _____

**19.** Relationship between two or more amounts of numbers     _____

**20.** Having a value that refers to something else     _____     /10

> Provide three examples of basic requirements for living, with support from the article.

**21.** Example 1: _____

Evidence: _____

**22.** Example 2: _____

Evidence: _____

**23.** Example 3: _____

Evidence: _____     /3

> Answer the following questions.

**24.** How does the article define 'extreme' poverty? _____

_____

**25.** Which part of the world has the greatest number of poor people? _____

**26.** What might prevent the MDG from achieving its target in 2015? _____

_____

**27.** Where in the world has the number of people living in poverty increased rather than

decreased? _____

**28.** Which community should become involved in reducing poverty?

_____

**29.** What reason does the article give for this community to become involved in reducing poverty? _____

_____

**30.** What two actions could this community do to work towards the goal of reducing extreme poverty and hunger?

_____

**31.** How could each of these actions support the goal? Use references from the article in your answer.

_____

_____

_____

_____

**32.** Why do you think the MDG is not aiming to completely eradicate poverty?

_____

**33.** Describe the living conditions of most alpaca farmers in Macusani.

_____

**34.** According to the article, are most alpaca farmers living in relative or absolute poverty?

_____

**35.** Explain your answer to question 34. _____

_____

**36.** What is the greatest concern of the alpaca farmers? _____

_____

**37.** What impact will the disappearance of the glacier on Mount Allinccapac have on the community? _____

**38.** How do you think this would affect the children who attend the local school?

_____

**39.** Who would be responsible for the disappearance of the glacier?

_____

**40.** What could rich countries do to prevent the negative impacts of the glacier?

_____

**41.** Why does the article include the account of Lucas Riquelme?

_____

**42.** What two factors are responsible for the food shortages in Ethiopia in 2008?

_____

**43.** Describe the DFID programme to help the most vulnerable people survive.

_____

**44.** Suggest one reason that the DFID programme did not help all the vulnerable people.

_____

**45.** What does Aster Kurma do five days a week? _____

**46.** Is it voluntary? Give a reason for your answer.

_____

**47.** How does the programme support what people like Aster Kurma need in the short term?

_____

**48.** How does the programme support what people like Aster Kurma need in the long term?

_____

**49.** What difficulties would Aster Kurma encounter if the programme did not exist?

_____

**50.** Why does the article include the account of Aster Kurma?

_____ /27

**51–65.** Complete the table for an essay plan to write a persuasive letter to your local Member of Parliament encouraging them to support the Millennium Development Goal to eradicate extreme poverty and hunger.

|  | Key Point | Evidence | Explanation |
|---|---|---|---|
| Introduction |  |  |  |
| Paragraph 1 |  |  |  |
| Paragraph 2 |  |  |  |
| Paragraph 3 |  |  |  |
| Conclusion |  |  |  |

/15

Explain why you would use the following five techniques in your letter.

**66.** Formal language: _____

**67.** Rhetorical questions: _____

**68.** Personal pronouns such as 'I', 'we', 'our', 'you': _____

**69.** Statistics: _____

**70.** Personalised accounts: _____

/5

/70

## PAPER 5

From The Times
February 4, 2010

### Fight Club: Is screen culture damaging our children's brains?

We ask two experts: Are video games and social networking websites hurting the next generation?

"Yes," says Baroness Greenfield, neuroscientist and director of the Institute for the Future of the Mind, the University of Oxford.

"Screen culture — video gaming and using computers in general — is impacting on our lives, especially those of the young, to an unprecedented degree. We know that the human brain        5
is exquisitely sensitive to the environment. It follows that if that environment is changing in unprecedented ways, so the brain may be changing in a way that results in a departure in mindset from that which human beings have had since we evolved.

First among these changes is a shorter attention span. If the young brain is exposed to a world of new images flashing up with each press of a key, then it might become accustomed        10
to operating over such timescales. Perhaps when, back in the real world, such responses are not forthcoming, attention deficit hyperactivity disorder will result.

Second, there is "living for the moment", where the emphasis is on sensory-laden thrill — the buzz of, say, rescuing the princess in a game. This is a literal world where everything is not related to previous experiences or any wider context. No care is given for the princess herself,  15
for the significance of her situation. Because there is none.

Third, recklessness. If most of a young child's actions take place on screen and so have no permanent consequences, it will prove a bad lesson when it comes to real life. A recent study found that obese people, for whom the sensual pleasure of eating trumps the consequences, are more reckless in performing tasks that involve an element of gambling. Could a daily life    20
lived in the two dimensions of the screen be similarly predisposing the brain to a disregard for consequences?

Fourth, a decline in the capacity for empathy. Interacting in person with others, listening to stories and reading novels are all good ways of learning about how others feel and think. The prolonged exposure to screen activities will, for the first time, stymie this familiar        25
developmental process.

Fifth, the diminished use of metaphor and abstract concepts. It would be difficult to expect current software to help the user to gain a sense of concepts such as honour, or of measuring one's life in coffee spoons (as mentioned by T. S. Eliot's Prufrock). Small children have problems interpreting metaphor. Might constant exposure to a literal world mean that the brain  30
remains infant-like?

Finally, there is the impact on our identity, which has been shaped by a narrative that we call our life story. If we live perpetually in the moment, and in a world where events are not linked consequentially, then might our sense of self be in jeopardy? The popularity of Twitter might indicate a need for feedback to remind us that we actually exist as unique and continuing entities.  35

Interestingly enough, the mindset profiled above is similar to that seen in a disparate range of conditions such as compulsive gambling and schizophrenia, and has been linked to an underactive prefrontal cortex. This area of the brain only becomes fully active in our late teens. My suggestion is that prolonged screen-based activities could be driving the malleable brain circuitry into a "hypo-frontal" state of persistent infancy." 40

"No", says Vaughan Bell, neuropsychologist at King's College London and the University of Antioquia, Colombia.

"I don't play computer games and I avoid Facebook but the scientific evidence doesn't support my personal prejudices. To date, research has shown that the internet is largely benign and that computer games are probably beneficial to the brains of young people. 45

In recent months, two scientific articles have reviewed the evidence on whether computer games cause problems in the workings of the brain and whether internet use is associated with mental health problems. Let's be clear that these articles do not represent surprising new findings; they are reviews of the many existing studies that help us understand whether screen culture is genuinely damaging the mind and brain. 50

In the journal *Current Directions in Psychological Science*, the cognitive scientist Matthew Dye, now at the University of Urbana-Champaign in Illinois, and colleagues reviewed studies of the effects of action video games, evaluated using standard neuropsychological tests. The unambiguous conclusions were that video gamers had quicker reactions than non-gamers, and that this edge was not achieved at the expense of being impulsive or making more 55 mistakes.

In other words gamers' brains worked faster, with no loss of accuracy, and there was no difference in levels of concentration or in the ability to resist quick but rash decisions.

Internet use has often been the focus of media scare stories, but once again there is little to worry about. A review published last year in *CyberPsychology and Behavior* by the 60 psychologist Chiungjung Huang, of the National Changhua University of Education in Taiwan, found that internet use was linked to a slight reduction in people's sense of wellbeing, but one so slender as to be irrelevant. What's more, there was no correlation with age.

Despite sensationalist headlines suggesting that social networking sites such as Facebook and MySpace lead to social problems, research on young people shows that use of the 65 sites is associated with a better social life in the real world because they use the services to enhance their existing relationships — just as anyone would do with the telephone.

Scare stories are attractive in part because they reflect our anxieties about new technology. But the idea that screen culture could be producing brain damage in children, and that people who deny the "brain-scrambling" potential of screen technology are like those who denied the 70 link between smoking and lung cancer, is brazen scaremongering.

There is an important debate to be had about the impact of technology on our lives, but personal opinion is no substitute for hard evidence, and as scientists we do the public a disservice if we confuse the two."

Read the passage then answer the following questions.

Match the definitions to the words in the box and state which line each word appears in.

| empathy | benign | scaremongering | malleable | perpetual |
|---|---|---|---|---|
| predisposing | diminished | entities | unprecedented | stymie |

1. never happened before _____

2. reduced _____

3. understanding of someone else's feelings _____

4. easily influenced _____

5. make somebody likely to do something _____

6. objects _____

7. slow down the progress of somebody or something _____

8. spreading shocking rumours _____

9. everlasting _____

10. kind _____

/10

Suggest synonyms for the words or phrases in bold in the following sentences.

11. 'In other words gamers' brains worked faster, with no loss of accuracy, and there was no difference in levels of concentration or in the ability to resist quick but **rash** decisions.'

_____

12. 'The **unambiguous** conclusions were that video gamers had quicker reactions than non-gamers...' _____

13. 'The **prolonged** exposure to screen activities will, for the first time, stymie this familiar developmental process.' _____

14. 'Despite **sensationalist** headlines suggesting that social networking sites such as Facebook and MySpace lead to social problems' _____

15. 'I don't play computer games and I avoid Facebook but the scientific evidence doesn't support my personal **prejudices**.' _____

16. 'We know that the human brain is **exquisitely** sensitive to the environment.'

_____

17. 'Could a daily life lived in the two dimensions of the screen be similarly predisposing the brain to **a disregard for** consequences?' _____

18. 'Third, **recklessness**. If most of a young child's actions take place on screen and so have no permanent consequences, it will prove a bad lesson when it comes to real life.'

_____

19. 'Interestingly enough, the mindset profiled above is similar to that seen in a **disparate** range of conditions.' _____

20. 'Scare stories are attractive in part because they reflect our **anxieties** about new technology.' _____

/10

Complete the table to summarise the key points in support of the argument.

| Point in support of the argument (in your own words) | Textual evidence |
|---|---|
| 21. | 22. |
| 23. | 24. |
| 25. | 26. |
| 27. | 28. |
| 29. | 30. |
| 31. | 32. |
| 33. | 34. |

/14

Complete the table to summarise the key points against the argument.

| Point against the argument (in your own words) | Textual evidence |
|---|---|
| 35. | 36. |
| 37. | 38. |
| 39. | 40. |
| 41. | 42. |
| 43. | 44. |
| 45. | 46. |
| 47. | 48. |

Answer the following questions.

/14

49. Why do you think the article includes the job titles for Baroness Greenfield and Vaughan Bell? _____

50. How responsive does Baroness Greenfield suggest the human brain is to the environment?
_____

51. What changes have been recorded in the way the human brain has evolved?
_____
_____

52. What problems does Baroness Greenfield see in 'living for the moment'?
_____
_____

53. What negative lesson does she suggest 'living for the moment' will teach young people?
_____
_____

**54.** Why does Baroness Greenfield suggest that we are losing the capacity to understand others? _____

_____

**55.** What does Baroness Greenfield suggest that Twitter shows a need for?

_____

_____

**56.** What are the five features of the mindset profile Baroness Greenfield offers?

_____

_____

**57.** What kind of profile does Baroness Greenfield suggest that this mindset profile is similar to?

_____

_____

**58.** Simplify the sentence: 'My suggestion is that prolonged screen-based activities could be driving the malleable brain circuitry into a "hypo-frontal" state of persistent infancy.'

_____

_____

**59.** What did the article say about whether computer games cause problems?

_____

_____

**60.** Why does Vaughan Bell claim that internet use is nothing to worry about?

_____

_____

**61.** Who does Vaughan Bell suggest is responsible for the increasing level of concern regarding internet use and game play?

_____

_____

**62.** What does Vaughan Bell state that scientists must never do?

_____

_____ /14

Write an extended paragraph comparing the two points of view.
You should include the following points in your answer.

- Comparison of the use of pronouns

- Formality of language

- Use of hard evidence

- The use of **modal auxiliaries** such as can, may, might, will.

- The use of linking adverbs

- Which point of view is more persuasive

- Justification of why the point of view chosen is more persuasive.

- Your own point of view with reasons.

**63–70.** _____

_____

_____

_____

_____

_____

_____

_____

_____

_____

_____

_____

/8

_____

/70

## PAPER 6

### 'Frankenstein' Chapter 5, by Mary Shelley

It was on a dreary night of November that I beheld the accomplishment of my toils. With an anxiety that almost amounted to agony, I collected the instruments of life around me, that I might infuse a spark of being into the lifeless thing that lay at my feet. It was already one in the morning; the rain pattered dismally against the panes, and my candle was nearly burnt out, when, by the glimmer of the half-extinguished light, I saw the dull yellow eye of the creature open; it breathed hard, and a convulsive motion agitated its limbs.   5

How can I describe my emotions at this catastrophe, or how delineate the wretch whom with such infinite pains and care I had endeavoured to form? His limbs were in proportion, and I had selected his features as beautiful. Beautiful! Great God! His yellow skin scarcely covered the work of muscles and arteries beneath; his hair was of a lustrous black, and flowing; his   10 teeth of a pearly whiteness; but these luxuriances only formed a more horrid contrast with his watery eyes, that seemed almost of the same colour as the dun-white sockets in which they were set, his shrivelled complexion and straight black lips.

The different accidents of life are not so changeable as the feelings of human nature. I had worked hard for nearly two years, for the sole purpose of infusing life into an inanimate   15 body. For this I had deprived myself of rest and health. I had desired it with an ardour that far exceeded moderation; but now that I had finished, the beauty of the dream vanished, and breathless horror and disgust filled my heart. Unable to endure the aspect of the being I had created, I rushed out of the room and continued a long time traversing my bed-chamber, unable to compose my mind to sleep. At length lassitude succeeded to the tumult I had   20 before endured, and I threw myself on the bed in my clothes, endeavouring to seek a few moments of forgetfulness. But it was in vain; I slept, indeed, but I was disturbed by the wildest dreams. I thought I saw Elizabeth, in the bloom of health, walking in the streets of Ingolstadt. Delighted and surprised, I embraced her, but as I imprinted the first kiss on her lips, they became livid with the hue of death; her features appeared to change, and I thought that I held   25 the corpse of my dead mother in my arms; a shroud enveloped her form, and I saw the grave-worms crawling in the folds of the flannel. I started from my sleep with horror; a cold dew covered my forehead, my teeth chattered, and every limb became convulsed; when, by the dim and yellow light of the moon, as it forced its way through the window shutters, I beheld the wretch—the miserable monster whom I had created. He held up the curtain of the bed;   30 and his eyes, if eyes they may be called, were fixed on me. His jaws opened, and he muttered some inarticulate sounds, while a grin wrinkled his cheeks. He might have spoken, but I did not hear; one hand was stretched out, seemingly to detain me, but I escaped and rushed downstairs. I took refuge in the courtyard belonging to the house which I inhabited, where I remained during the rest of the night, walking up and down in the greatest agitation, listening   35 attentively, catching and fearing each sound as if it were to announce the approach of the demoniacal corpse to which I had so miserably given life.

Read the passage then answer the following questions.

Match each word in the box from the passage to its correct definition below.

| hue | demoniacal | livid | tumult | lassitude | compose | traversing |
| --- | --- | --- | --- | --- | --- | --- |
| ardour | proportion | aspect | catastrophe | infinite | lustrous | |
| endeavour | delineate | convulsive | agitate | extinguish | infuse | toil |

1. try very hard _____

2. sudden jerky movements _____

3. without any limits _____

4. shining _____

5. bruised colour _____

6. put out fire or light _____

7. hard work _____

8. image _____

9. make someone feel anxious or nervous _____

10. fill up with _____

11. passion _____

12. crossing _____

13. relative size _____

14. calm _____

15. disaster _____

16. describe _____

17. like an evil spirit _____

18. a shade of colour _____

19. tiredness _____

20. a mental state of anxiety _____

/20

Choose the correct prefix or suffix from the box for each of the words below. Write the new word on the answer line.

| hood | micro | auto | ship | ess |
|------|-------|------|------|-----|
| inter | dis | ism | er | in |

**21.** complete _____

**22.** national _____

**23.** biography _____

**24.** meter _____

**25.** loyal _____

**26.** brother _____

**27.** friend _____

**28.** lion _____

**29.** London _____

**30.** romantic _____

/10

Rewrite the following sentences to make them sound more modern.

**31.** 'It was on a dreary night of November that I beheld the accomplishment of my toils.'

_____

**32.** 'It was already one in the morning; the rain pattered dismally against the panes, and my candle was nearly burnt out…'

_____

_____

**33.** 'How can I describe my emotions at this catastrophe, or how delineate the wretch whom with such infinite pains and care I had endeavoured to form?'

_____

_____

**34.** 'For this I had deprived myself of rest and health.'

_____

**35.** At length lassitude succeeded to the tumult I had before endured, and I threw myself on the bed in my clothes, endeavouring to seek a few moments of forgetfulness.

_____

_____

/5

> Put the following summary statements of the text in the correct order from 1 to 10.

| | | |
|---|---|---|
| **36.** | Frankenstein ran away from the creature to his bedroom and tried to settle his mind to sleep. | |
| **37.** | Frankenstein was bitterly disappointed by his experiment and sickened by the creature. | |
| **38.** | Frankenstein had a nightmare that Elizabeth turned into the buried body of his dead mother. | |
| **39.** | One night in November, Frankenstein nervously arranged his medical instruments. | |
| **40.** | The creature came into Frankenstein's bedroom and held out his arm to Frankenstein. | |
| **41.** | Around one in the morning, the creature opened his eyes and his body shook. | |
| **42.** | Frankenstein ran away from the monster and walked up and down for the rest of the night. | |
| **43.** | Frankenstein had worked for two years on his greatest ambition which was to create life. | |
| **44.** | The creature's appearance was horrifying to Frankenstein. | |
| **45.** | Frankenstein dreamt of kissing Elizabeth's lips which turned them to the colour of death. | |

/10

Answer these questions.

**46.** Why does Shelley use the first person point of view in this chapter?

_____

**47.** In which lines does Shelley make Frankenstein address the reader directly?

_____    /2

Choose a quotation from the passage to support
each of the following statements about the text.

**48.** Frankenstein's ambition was to create life from a non-living form.

_____

_____

**49.** Frankenstein did not look after himself when he was working hard to achieve his ambition.

_____

_____

**50.** Frankenstein was sickened with the result of his efforts.

_____

_____

**51.** Frankenstein thinks he has created an evil monster.

_____

_____

**52.** The creature wants to communicate with Frankenstein, his creator.

_____

_____    /5

State whether the following statements about **gothic stories** are true or false.

53. A gothic story will have lots of imagery relating to darkness. _____

54. Gothic stories often include supernatural elements. _____

55. Gothic stories are always about love and marriage. _____

56. Gothic stories are usually set in wild landscapes. _____

57. Gothic stories never contain nightmares. _____

58. Gothic stories are often about death and decay. _____

59. Gothic novels often have more than one narrator. _____

60. Gothic novels always end happily. _____     /8

Choose the correct figurative technique from the box for each of the quotations below. Write the technique on the answer line.

| **pathetic fallacy** | **metaphor** | **positive imagery** |
| --- | --- | --- |
| | **contrasting imagery** | **images of death** |

61. 'a shroud enveloped her form' _____

62. 'half-extinguished light' _____

63. 'the rain pattered dismally against the panes' _____

64. 'I saw the grave-worms crawling in the folds of the flannel.' _____

65. 'his hair was of a lustrous black, and flowing; his teeth of a pearly whiteness' _____

66. 'demoniacal corpse' _____

67. 'in the bloom of health' _____

68. 'I collected the instruments of life around me' _____     /10

69. 'dim and yellow light of the moon' _____

70. 'His yellow skin scarcely covered the work of muscles
    and arteries beneath' _____     /70

## PAPER 7

**'Antigone'** by Sophocles

Antigone is the maid who is mentioned in Line 9 of the scene below.
Before the scene starts, Antigone has buried her brother who was a traitor.
This was against the command of Creon, the King, and as punishment, he sentences
Antigone to death.

CHORUS: If he says anything appropriate, listen to him, King.
(To HAEMON) Listen thou thy sire too; both have spoken well.
CREON: What, would you have us at our age be schooled,
Lessoned in caution by a beardless boy?
HAEMON: I beg for justice, father, nothing more.                          5
Weigh me upon my merit, not my years.
CREON: Strange merit this to approve lawlessness!
HAEMON: For evil-doers I would urge no plea.
CREON: Is not this maid an outright law-breaker?
HAEMON: The Theban commons with one voice say, No.                         10
CREON: What, shall the mob dictate my policy?
HAEMON: 'Tis thou, methinks, who speakest like a boy.
CREON: Am I to rule for others, or myself?
HAEMON: A State for one man is no State at all.
CREON: The State is his who rules it, so 'tis said.                        15
HAEMON: As monarch of a desert thou wouldst shine.
CREON: This boy, methinks, upholds the woman's cause.
HAEMON: If thou be a woman, yes. My thought's for thee.
CREON: O rascal, would'st battle with thy sire?
HAEMON: Because I see thee wrongfully wicked.                              20
CREON: And am I wrong, if I keep my rights?
HAEMON: Talk not of rights; thou spurn'st the due of Heaven
CREON: O heart corrupt, a woman's slave thou!
HAEMON: Slave to dishonour thou wilt never find me.
CREON: Thy speech at least was all a plea for her.                        25
HAEMON: And thee and me, and for the gods below.
CREON: Living, the maid shall never be thy bride.
HAEMON: So she shall die, but I will die with her.
CREON: Has't come to such a pass as threaten me?
HAEMON: What threat is this, vain counsels to accuse?                     30
CREON: Vain fool to instruct thy betters; thou shall rue it.
HAEMON: Were you not my father, I had said thou err'st.
CREON: Play not the spaniel, thou a woman's slave.
HAEMON: When thou dost speak, must no man make reply?
CREON: This passes boundaries. By heaven, thou shalt not rate             35

And jeer and flout me without regard.
Off with the hateful thing that she may die
At once, beside her bridegroom, in his sight.
HAEMON: Think not that in my sight the maid shall die,
Or by my side; never shalt thou again                                    40
Behold my face hereafter. Go, consort
With friends who like a madman for their mate.
[Exit HAEMON]

> Read the extract from the play then answer the following questions.

Choose the most powerful synonym from the box for each of the words in bold below.

| | | | | |
|---|---|---|---|---|
| intimidate | implore | odd | taught | entreaty |
| conceited | complete | sovereign | outlandish | big-headed |
| lecture | guided | immoral | request | talk |
| absolute | bully | bad | ask | ruler |

**1.** CREON: What, would you have us at our age be **schooled**…  _____

**2.** HAEMON: I **beg** for justice, father, nothing more.  _____

**3.** CREON: **Strange** merit this to approve lawlessness!  _____

**4.** CREON: Is not this maid an **outright** law-breaker?  _____

**5.** HAEMON: As **monarch** of a desert thou wouldst shine.  _____

**6.** HAEMON: Because I see thee wrongfully **wicked**.  _____

**7.** CREON: Thy speech at least was all a **plea** for her.  _____

**8.** CREON: Thy **speech** at least was all a plea for her  _____

**9.** CREON: Has't come to such a pass as **threaten** me?  _____

**10.** CREON: **Vain** fool to instruct thy betters; thou shall rue it.  _____

/10

Rewrite the following lines, changing the words in bold to make the line simple and informal.

11. Listen **thou thy sire** too; both have spoken well.

_____

12. '**Tis thou, methinks**, who **speakest** like a boy.

_____

13. As **monarch** of a desert **thou wouldst** shine.

_____

14. If thou be a woman, yes. My **thought's** for **thee**.

_____

15. O rascal, **would'st** battle with **thy sire**?

_____

16. And **thee** and me, and for the gods below.

_____

17. **Has't** come to such a pass as threaten me?

_____

18. Living, the maid shall never be **thy** bride.

_____

19. Vain fool to instruct **thy** betters; **thou** shall **rue** it.

_____

20. When **thou dost** speak, must no man make reply?

_____    /10

Answer these questions.

21. What is the relationship between Haemon and Creon? _____

22. Choose two lines from the text to support your answer to question 21.

_____

_____

**23.** What is the subject of the speech? _____

**24.** What does Haemon want Creon to do? _____

**25.** What advice does the Chorus give to Creon?

_____

**26.** Why does Creon say, "What, would you have us at our age be schooled, Lessoned in caution by a beardless boy?"

_____

**27.** Do you think the Chorus is closer in age to Creon or to Haemon? _____

**28.** Find a quotation to support your answer to question 27.

_____

**29.** What do you think the relationship is between the Chorus and Creon?

_____

**30.** Find a quotation to support your answer to question 29.

_____

**/10**

## Fill in the blanks in these sentences.

**31.** _____ believes that the maid has committed a crime.

**32.** _____ believes that the maid has not committed a crime.

**/2**

## Answer these questions.

**33.** Creon asks, "Am I to rule for others, or myself?" What type of question is this?

_____

**34.** Haemon answers Creon with, "A State for one man is no State at all." Explain his answer.

_____

**35.** Creon's reply to Haemon is a statement; "The state is his who rules it, so t'is said." Does this show that Creon rules for his people or for himself?

_____

**36.** Haemon's response is, "As monarch of a desert thou wouldst shine." What does he mean by this? _____

**37.** Which two words have a connected meaning in, 'As monarch of a desert thou wouldst shine.'? _____

**38.** Explain how the words in your answer to question 37 are connected.

_____

/6

Find four words in the text that are related to kingship.

**39.** _____ spoken by _____

**40.** _____ spoken by _____

**41.** _____ spoken by _____

/4

**42.** _____ spoken by _____

List the curses that Creon calls Haemon.

**43.** _____

**44.** _____

**45.** _____

**46.** _____

/5

**47.** _____

Answer these questions.

**48.** What kind of personal qualities would you expect a ruler to have? List three.

_____

**49.** Find the first reference in the text that demonstrates that Haemon thinks Creon is evil.

_____

**50.** What punishment for the maid has Creon decided? _____

**51.** Find a quotation to support your answer to question 50.

_____

**52.** What punishment for Haemon has Creon decided? _____

**53.** Find a quotation to support your answer to question 52.

_____

**54.** Why does the structure of the speech change in the last eight lines?

_____

**55.** Why do you think the dramatist has given Haemon the last four lines?

_____ /8

**56–70.** Write the outline of an essay in response to the question: How does Sophocles persuade the audience that Haemon is right in this extract?

For each paragraph you should write the outline of a:

- Point
- Evidence
- Explanation

Introduction: Lines 1–10: How does the dramatist set the scene?

**56.** Point:

_____

**57.** Evidence:

_____

**58.** Explanation:

_____

_____

Point 1: Lines 11–20: What key theme is introduced in this extract?

**59.** Point:

_____

**60.** Evidence:

_____

**61.** Explanation:

_____

_____

Point 3: Lines 21–34: How does Sophocles make Haemon's argument personal and emotional?

**62.** Point:

_____

**63.** Evidence:

_____

**64.** Explanation:

_____

_____

Point 4: Lines 35–38: Why does Sophocles turn the audience against Creon?

**65.** Point:

_____

**66.** Evidence:

_____

**67.** Explanation:

_____

_____

Point 5: Lines 39–42: How does Sophocles create sympathy for Haemon and his point of view?

**68.** Point:

_____

**69.** Evidence:

_____

**70.** Explanation:

_____

_____

/15

/70

## PAPER 8

### 'Remember' by Christina Rossetti

Remember me when I am gone away,
Gone far away into the silent land;
When you can no more hold me by the hand,
Nor I half turn to go yet turning stay.
Remember me when no more day by day                      5
You tell me of our future that you plann'd:
Only remember me; you understand
It will be late to counsel then or pray.
Yet if you should forget me for a while
And afterwards remember, do not grieve:                  10
For if the darkness and corruption leave
A vestige of the thoughts that once I had,
Better by far you should forget and smile
Than that you should remember and be sad.                14

### 'Sonnets from the Portuguese'

### 'XLIII' by Elizabeth Barrett-Browning

How do I love thee? Let me count the ways.
I love thee to the depth and breadth and height
My soul can reach, when feeling out of sight
For the ends of Being and ideal Grace.
I love thee to the level of everyday's                   5
Most quiet need, by sun and candle-light.
I love thee freely, as men strive for Right;
I love thee purely, as they turn from Praise.
I love thee with the passion put to use
In my old grief, and with my childhood's faith.          10
I love thee with a love I seemed to lose
With my lost saints,–I love thee with the breath,
Smiles, tears, of all my life !–and, if God choose,
I shall but love thee better after death.                14

Read the two poems then answer the questions.

The following questions relate to Christina Rossetti's poem 'Remember'.

1. Identify the narrative viewpoint. _____

/1

2–4. Write a paragraph explaining why this narrative viewpoint is effective. You should include the following points in your paragraph:

- Main Point
- Evidence in the form of an embedded quotation
- Analysis of the language or literary techniques used in the quotation.

_____

_____

_____

_____

/3

Answer these questions.

5. Where is the persona going? _____

6. Does the persona reveal when they are going to this place? Give a reason for your answer.

_____

7. Generally, what does the persona ask her lover to do in the first six lines?

/3

_____

When specifically, does the persona ask her lover to remember her in the first six lines? Find the quotations.

8. Request 1: _____

9. Request 2: _____

10. Request 3: _____

11. Request 4: _____

/4

Answer these questions.

**12.** Describe the effect of the semi-colon in line 7.

_____

**13.** Why will it be too late for her lover to 'counsel' or 'pray' as stated in line 8?

_____

**14.** Identify the line where the persona changes the tone. _____

**15.** Explain why the tone of the poem changes at this point in the poem.

_____

**16.** What two conflicting emotions does Rossetti present in the poem?

_____          /5

**17–20.** Write a paragraph describing the language Rossetti uses to refer to death.
You should include the following points in your paragraph:
  • Main point
  • Evidence in the form of an embedded quotation
  • Explanation
  • Analysis of the language or literary techniques used in the quotation.

_____

_____

_____

_____

_____          /4

**21–24.** Write a paragraph describing how Rossetti presents the two emotions in the poem. You
should include the following points in your paragraph.
  • Main point
  • Evidence in the form of an embedded quotation
  • Explanation
  • Analysis of the language or literary techniques used in the quotation.

_____

_____

_____

_____          /4

_____

Answer the following questions in relation to Elizabeth Barrett-Browning's poem 'XLIII'.

**25.** Identify the narrative viewpoint Barrett-Browning uses in the poem.

_____

**26.** State why the narrative viewpoint the poet has chosen is appropriate for the content of the poem.

_____  /2

Identify the eight reasons Barrett-Browning gives in response to the question, 'How do I love thee?'

**27.** _____

**28.** _____

**29.** _____

**30.** _____

**31.** _____

**32.** _____

**33.** _____

**34.** _____  /8

Answer these questions.

**35.** Identify the rhyme scheme in the poem. _____

**36.** What is the form of the poem? _____

**37.** Why do you think that this form is appropriate? _____

_____

**38.** What is the pattern of the rhythm in the poem? _____

**39.** Why do you think that this form of rhythm is appropriate? _____

_____

**40.** Using an embedded quotation, how would you describe the tone of the poem?

_____

_____

**41.** Which theme, love or death, does Barrett-Browning give more emphasis to?

_____

**42–45.** Write a paragraph summarising how Barrett-Browning presents love in her poem. You should include the following points in your paragraph:

- Main point
- Evidence on the form of an embedded quotation
- Explanation
- Analysis of the language or literary techniques used in the quotation.

/7

_____

_____

_____

_____

_____

/4

**46–70.** Write the outline of an essay in response to the question: 'Compare the way Christina Rossetti and Elizabeth Barrett-Browning present love and death in their poems.' For each paragraph, you should write the outline of your:

- Point
- Evidence
- Explanation of the evidence supporting your point
- Analysis of language or literary techniques.

**Introduction**

**46.** Point:

_____

**47.** Evidence:

_____

**48.** Explanation:

_____

_____

**49.** Analysis of language or literary techniques:

_____

_____ /4

**Paragraph 1**

**50.** Point:

_____

**51.** Evidence:

_____

**52.** Explanation:

_____

_____

**53.** Analysis of language or literary techniques:

_____

_____ /4

**Paragraph 2**

**54.** Point:

_____

**55.** Evidence:

_____

**56.** Explanation:

_____

_____

**57.** Analysis of language or literary techniques:

_____

_____ /4

**Paragraph 3**

**58.** Point:

_____

**59.** Evidence:

_____

**60.** Explanation:

_____

_____

**61.** Analysis of language or literary techniques:

_____

_____ ( **/4** )

**Paragraph 4**

  **62.** Point:

_____

  **63.** Evidence:

_____

  **64.** Explanation:

_____

_____

  **65.** Analysis of language or literary techniques:

_____

_____ ( **/4** )

**Conclusion**

  **66.** Point (refers back to introduction):

_____

  **67.** Evidence:

_____

  **68.** Explanation:

_____

_____

  **69.** Analysis of language or literary techniques:

_____

_____ ( **/5** )

  **70.** Personal viewpoint about the poems:

_____ ( **/70** )

_____

## PAPER 9

From The Sunday Times
October 4, 2009

### D'oh! Homer Simpson to teach us healthy living

Sarah-Kate Templeton, Health Editor

HOMER SIMPSON is known for munching doughnuts and swigging beer, but the Department of Health has decided that his family's lifestyle is healthy enough to enlist them in an anti-obesity campaign.

The government is to sponsor episodes of the cartoon serial about the dysfunctional family for three months in an attempt to improve the nation's diet and increase exercise levels. 5

Officials hope that families slumped in front of the Channel 4 programme will see a reflection of themselves in The Simpsons and realise they should probably be taking more care of their health. 10

Critics may suggest that there are better examples of healthy lifestyles — such as the cartoon character Sportacus, who encourages the children of Lazytown to eat more fruit.

Despite appearances, however, ministers believe much of the Simpsons' lifestyle could set a good example to British families.

Officials analysed the Simpsons' dietary and exercise patterns and believe Homer's son, 15
Bart, achieves the government-recommended 60 minutes of exercise a day. Bart's sister, Lisa, is a vegetarian and is likely to consume the daily target of five portions of fruit and vegetables. For example, they eat together round the dining table and are a caring and sharing family, despite their many troubles.

At the beginning of episodes viewers will see cartoon characters pretending to be Homer, 20
Bart, Marge and the rest of the family sitting on the sofa eating their favourite snacks of pizza, ice cream and chips.

The characters, designed for the Change4Life campaign by Aardman Animations, creators of Wallace and Gromit, will then see all the junk food disappear to be replaced with more nutritious fare such as carrots, apples and pears. 25

Gillian Merron, the public health minister, said: "The Simpsons are a much-loved, close-knit family facing some of the everyday challenges that modern-day families go through. They provide a popular and engaging way to get the message to real-life families about simple ways of improving their diet and activity for a healthier lifestyle."

The health department acknowledges that the Simpsons' lifestyle is not entirely healthy 30
and this is reflected in the slogan for the £640,000 advertising campaign: "Supporting The Simpsons: Sometimes."

A spokeswoman added: "The beer-drinking and doughnut-eating is clearly not what we would want."

Sponsors of The Simpsons included Domino's Pizza until Ofcom, the communications 35
regulator, ruled it was in breach of the broadcasting code because the commercials advertised junk food to children.

Professor Gerard Hastings, director of the institute for social marketing at Stirling University, believes the public is more likely to listen to healthy-living tips if they come from imperfect characters. 40

"It is good that health is associated with something irreverent and fun instead of po-faced and worthy," said Hastings. "It is not what is said but who says it that matters and the fact that Homer and Bart Simpson are implicitly endorsing this message is really important.

"We all have within us a bit of the beer and doughnuts persona and, within reason, that is fine. It is about balance and moderation. 45

"What this will hopefully do is advertise that being healthy does not automatically put you into that miserable, Calvinist group."

Obesity is estimated to cost the NHS £4.2 billion a year and this is set to more than double by 2050. Forecasts suggest that a fifth of children will be overweight or obese by next year.

> Read the article then answer the following questions.

Match the words in the box to the definitions below and state which line they appear in.

| | | | |
|---|---|---|---|
| breach | endorse | dysfunctional | consume |
| regulator | slumped | acknowledge | |
| irreverent | enlist | implicitly | |

**1.** Gain the support of _____

**2.** To eat or drink something _____

**3.** Lacking in respect _____

**4.** Drooping posture _____

**5.** Unable to function emotionally in a social unit _____

**6.** Not stated explicitly _____

**7.** Failure to keep a promise or law _____

**8.** An official body that controls an activity _____

**9.** Give approval for something _____

**10.** To admit or recognise something _____

/10

Answer the following questions.

**11.** What is the Department of Health campaigning for? _____

**12.** Why is the Department of Health campaigning for this? Give three reasons provided by the article. _____

**13.** What two things will the campaign encourage?

_____

**14.** What do officials hope people will recognise when watching The Simpsons?

_____

**15–18.** List the two Simpsons characters that will do most to support the campaign, and give a reason for each answer.

Character 1: _____

Reason: _____

Character 2: _____

Reason: _____

**19.** Which two characters are suggested by a comment in the article as the most imperfect?

_____

**20.** Why will these two imperfect characters mean that the Healthy Living campaign will be effective? _____

/10

Complete the summary table of points that support the
Department of Health's decision to sponsor The Simpsons.

| Point | Evidence (line reference) | Explanation |
|---|---|---|
| 21. | 22. | 23. |
| 24. | 25. | 26. |
| 27. | 28. | 29. |
| 30. | 31. | 32. |
| 33. | 34. | 35. |
| 36. | 37. | 38. |
| 39. | 40. | 41. |
| 42. | 43. | 44. |
| 45. | 46. | 47. |

/27

Answer the following questions.

**48.** What is surprising about the Department of Health's decision to sponsor The Simpsons?

_____

**49.** What reason do they give for their decision? _____

**50.** How have some people been critical of the decision? _____

**51.** Why does Domino's Pizza no longer sponsor The Simpsons?

_____

/4

Find examples from the text of the following techniques.

**52.** Listing of three: _____

**53.** Alliteration: _____

**54.** Contrasting statement: _____

**55.** Cliché: _____

/4

Summarise the comments made by the people quoted in the article.
Suggest whether they are for or against the Department of Health's
decision to sponsor The Simpsons, and evaluate their use of language.

**The Minister for Public Health**

**56.** Summary of comment: _____

**57.** For or against? _____

**58.** Evaluation of comment: _____

**Department of Health**

**59.** Summary of comment: _____

**50.** For or against? _____

**61.** Evaluation of comment: _____

**Director of the Institute for Social Marketing at Stirling University**

**62.** Summary of comment: _____

**63.** For or against? _____

**64.** Evaluation of comment: _____  ( /9 )

**65–70.** Write a paragraph summarising whether you agree or disagree with the Department of Health's decision to sponsor The Simpsons ensuring that you use the following guidelines.

- Formal language
- Hard evidence such as figures or statistics
- Summary statement supporting the decision
- Summary statement rejecting the decision
- Your own point of view
- Provide reasons for your point of view.

_____

_____

_____

_____

_____

_____

_____

_____

_____

_____

_____  ( /6 )

_____

_____  ( /70 )

## PAPER 10

From The Times
February 2, 2010

# Joe Rollino: strongman, weightlifter and boxer.

Joe Rollino achieved something of the status of a superhero in
New York. Often known as the Great or Mighty Joe Rollino, or when
in the boxing ring as Kid Dundee, and when in his home quarter
familiarly nicknamed Puggy, he was the last of the Coney Island
strongmen.                                                                                    5

Rollino in his prime: he
was the last of the Coney
Island strongmen                                                                              10

Though relatively small in stature he was confidently billed in the
1920s as "The World's Strongest Man". That was an exaggeration,
but there is no doubt that he was a physical phenomenon, and he
is reckoned by students of physical culture to have been, for his
size, one of the strongest men who ever lived.

At the peak of his career he stood only 5ft 5in (1.65m) and weighed little more than 10st
(63kg), yet he lifted weights of 475lb (216kg) with his teeth, 635lb (288kg) with one finger,
1,500lb (682kg) in a hand-and-thigh lift, and 3,200lb (1,454kg) on his back. He did have a 20in
neck (51cm), and he once used it to raise a carousel with 14 people on it, to popular acclaim.

He swam in the Atlantic every day for years on end, whatever the temperature, and was credited     15
with having retrieved the bodies of two drowning victims in Prospect Park in a bitter 1950s
midwinter, when police lacked the protective equipment necessary for them to go in the water.

As a boxer, under the name Kid Dundee, Rollino had some 100 fights in the 1920s, and
though often fighting men weighing 50lb (22kg) more than him, claimed that no one could
ever knock him out. After retiring from the ring he worked as a longshoreman. On one                20
occasion he was hired to play a bit part in Elia Kazan's film On the Waterfront. His big scene,
though, ended up on the cutting room floor.

In the Second World War, while serving in the Pacific theatre, he was awarded three Purple
Hearts, a Silver Star and a Bronze star. Shards of shrapnel in his legs — "You could sell me
for scrap," he used to joke — did not stop him walking five miles every morning, rain or            25
shine. He abjured meat, cigarettes and alcohol and at the age of 104 was still capable of
bending coins with his teeth or his thumb, though he would apologise when thus deforming
a quarter that he used to be able to do it with a dime.

Joe Rollino was born in Coney Island, New York, in 1905. He was the son of Italian
immigrants and one of 14 children. He said he was "born strong", and he could show a                30
photograph of himself already in strong man pose at the age of 10.

His love affair with boxing started young: as a 14-year-old he was taken by one of his brothers to see Jack Dempsey box. Dempsey knocked out the gargantuan Jess Willard in Toledo, Ohio, and Rollino reckoned it was most exciting fight he ever saw, "and I've seen a lot of them".

Even as a centenarian Rollino shadow-boxed fluently, throwing combinations with aplomb,     35
parrying and dipping like a 25-year-old.

He was a longtime member and patriarch of the Association of Oldtime Barbell and Strongmen, an organisation of men given to such feats as bending steel spikes or nails with their bare hands and ripping books in half from the bound side. Even in such prodigious company it was conceded that Rollino, who still worked out regularly in the gym, was "in     40
pretty good shape", though "he walked a little slow".

Maybe that was his final undoing, for on the morning of Monday January 11, as he returned from fetching his morning paper as usual, the Great Joe Rollino was hit by a van while crossing Bay Ridge Parkway at 13th Avenue. He suffered fractures to his pelvis, chest, ribs and face, as well as head trauma, and though taken unconscious to Lutheran Medical     45
Centre, he died shortly after arrival. It is thought that he had never married, and he is survived by a niece with whom he lived in the last years of his life.

**Joe Rollino, strongman, weightlifter and boxer, was born on March 19, 1905. He died on January 11, 2010, aged 104.**

---

### Unscramble each set of letters to make a word related to physical activity.

**1.** Scrape quid     _____

**2.** Mars thing     _____

**3.** Act my sign     _____

**4.** Earn mutton     _____

**5.** Crept is     _____

**6.** Fly I qua     _____

**7.** Mi by toil     _____

**8.** Dim niece     _____

**9.** Hi cattle     _____

**10.** Gaily it     _____

/10

Suggest a definition and a synonym for each of the words in bold in the following sentences.

'Even in such **prodigious** company it was conceded that Rollino, who still worked out regularly in the gym, was "in pretty good shape", though "he walked a little slow".'

**11.** Definition: _____

**12.** Synonym: _____

'Even in such prodigious company it was **conceded** that Rollino, who still worked out regularly in the gym, was "in pretty good shape", though "he walked a little slow".'

**13.** Definition: _____

**14.** Synonym: _____

'Joe Rollino achieved something of the **status** of a superhero in New York.'

**15.** Definition: _____

**16.** Synonym: _____

'That was an exaggeration, but there is no doubt that he was a physical **phenomenon**…'

**17.** Definition: _____

**18.** Synonym: _____

'…he is **reckoned** by students of physical culture to have been, for his size, one of the strongest men who ever lived.'

**19.** Definition: _____

**20.** Synonym: _____

'…he once used it to raise a carousel with 14 people on it, to popular **acclaim.**'

**21.** Definition: _____

**22.** Synonym: _____

'[He] was credited with having **retrieved** the bodies of two drowning victims in Prospect Park in a bitter 1950s midwinter…'

**23.** Definition: _____

**24.** Synonym: _____

'He **abjured** meat, cigarettes and alcohol and at the age of 104 was still capable of bending coins with his teeth or his thumb…'

**25.** Definition: _____

**26.** Synonym: _____

'…he would apologise when thus **deforming** a quarter that he used to be able to do it with a dime.'

**27.** Definition: _____

**28.** Synonym: _____

'Even as a centenarian Rollino shadow-boxed fluently, throwing combinations with **aplomb,** parrying and dipping like a 25-year-old.'

**29.** Definition: _____

**30.** Synonym: _____                                    /20

### Answer these questions.

**31.** Why do you think that Joe Rollino was known by a nickname like "Puggy" in his home quarter when he was widely known as the "Mighty Joe Rollino"?

_____

**32.** Why is it surprising that he was billed as "The World's Strongest Man" in the 1920s?

_____

**33.** What does the use of the word 'confidently' in line 6 suggest?

_____

**34.** What facts quoted in the article support the assertion made by 'students of physical culture' that he was "for his size, one of the strongest men who ever lived."?

_____

**35.** What does the article suggest is Joe Rollino's most impressive achievement?

_____

**36.** What motivated Joe Rollino to box?

_____

**37.** From the information provided in the article, suggest why this made such an impact on Joe Rollino.

_____

**38–39.** How do you know that Joe Rollino did not take himself too seriously? Analyse a quotation to support your answer.

_____

_____

**40.** How old was Joe Rollino when he first became interested in his physical appearance?

_____

/10

Find examples of the following techniques and evaluate their effect in the extract.

Rule of three.

**41.** Example: _____

**42.** Evaluation: _____

_____

Rule of three.

**43.** Example: _____

**44.** Evaluation: _____

_____

Rule of three.

**45.** Example: _____

**46.** Evaluation _____

_____

Rule of three.

**47.** Example: _____

**48.** Evaluation _____

_____

Antithesis.

**49.** Example: _____

**50.** Evaluation _____

_____

Alliteration.

**51.** Example: _____

**52.** Evaluation _____

_____

Sentence using a **subordinating concession conjunction**.

**53.** Example:_____

**54.** Evaluation _____

_____

/14

> Answer these questions.

**55–56.** Explain why the article does not begin with any mention of biographical details? You should use embedded quotation(s) and provide an explanation for your use of quotation.

_____

_____

_____

**57.** Why did Joe Rollino apologise for deforming a quarter?

_____

**58.** What is interesting about the sentence construction of 'Shards of shrapnel in his legs — "You could sell me for scrap," he used to joke — did not stop him walking five miles every morning, rain or shine.'?

_____

**59.** How does the writer link this sentence (24–26) with the previous sentence, 'In the Second World War, while serving in the Pacific theatre, he was awarded three Purple Hearts, a Silver Star and a Bronze star.'?

_____

**60.** What is sadly ironic about the event described in the final paragraph?

_____

/6

**61–70.** How does the writer create the impression that Joe Rollino was a legend? You should include the following techniques in your answer.

- Refer to the writer's use of tense
- Use embedded textual references
- Use at least one compound sentence
- Use at least one semi-colon and correct punctuation
- Use a powerful opening sentence
- Refer to the writer's use of adjectives
- Refer to the writer's use of adverbs
- Use first person voice
- Refer to how the writer's last paragraph echoes the opening paragraph
- Include your personal viewpoint.

/10

/70

| | |
|---|---|
| **comedy** | a play that begins with a problem but ends happily |
| **complex sentence** | a sentence where the clauses are joined together by subordination or coordination or both |
| **complication** | a difficulty that occurs halfway through a fiction text |
| **contemporary** | a reference that can be understood by most people at the time it was written |
| **embedded quotation** | a quotation that is placed within a sentence |
| **emphasising conjuncts** | an adverb that links together clauses, sentences or paragraphs, e.g. *above all, in particular, especially* |
| **evaluation** | to assess how effective something is by providing evidence |
| **extract** | a smaller passage from a larger text |
| **gothic story** | a type of fiction that uses the themes of decay, violent action and grand, gloomy settings |
| **irony** | a situation or a statement that is deliberately presented as different to what is actually true |
| **modal auxiliaries** | a verb that is put before the main verb to show permission such as *could / would* |
| **myth** | an ancient story about heroes or supernatural beings |
| **pathetic fallacy** | the description of the external environment to show how a character is feeling |
| **persona** | a character in a play, novel or poem |
| **subordinating concession conjunction** | an adverb that suggests compromise, such as *although*, which connects a secondary clause to the main clause in a sentence |
| **tragedy** | a play that begins hopefully but ends sadly |

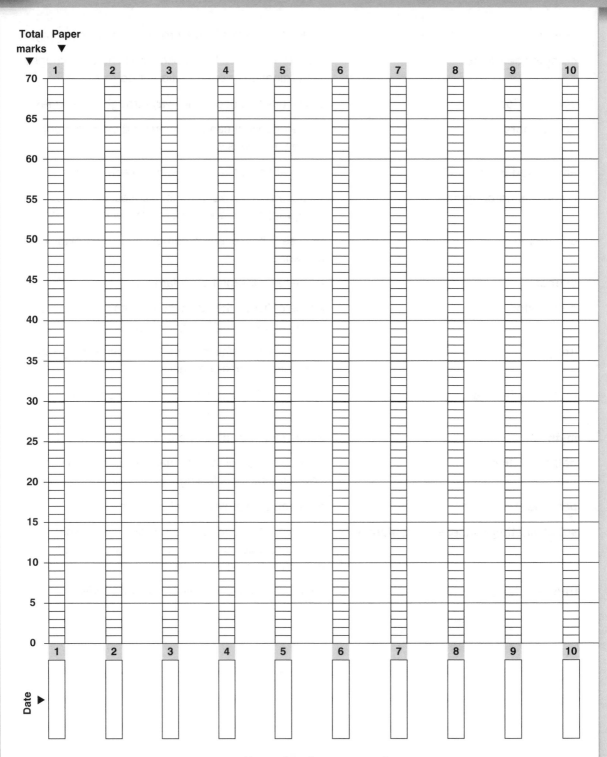

**Now colour in your score!**

# Answer booklet: KS3 English Levels 6–7

**Please Note:** Answers to questions which require explanation are given as guidance to the types of answers expected. Correct answers to these questions should contain the same meaning, but do not need to be word perfect with the example answers given.

## Paper 1

1. isolated / deserted
2. greatest
3. overjoyed, ecstatic
4. excellent, talented, skilled,
5. wept, sobbed, howled, bawled.

6–10.

| | |
|---|---|
| 'Hermes, the god of **persuasion,** gave her the powerful gift of the gab…' | → to be able to get somebody to do something |
| 'The last gift the gods gave her was a beautiful **ornate** gilded gold jar.' | → lots of detailed decoration |
| '"I'm not interested in your independent women, Prometheus. They all have too much to say for themselves." Epimetheus **retorted** haughtily.' | → to respond quickly in an insulting or sharp way |
| '"I'm not interested in your independent women, Prometheus. They all have too much to say for themselves." Epimetheus retorted **haughtily**.' | → to behave in a self-important way |
| 'Lots of tiny dark wings battered at Pandora, they were all the evils things of the world; jealousy, hatred, revenge, diseases and disasters, cruelty and **malice**.' | → the wish to do harm or cause pain to someone |

11. Zeus, the god of all gods, told Hephaestus to make the most beautiful girl in the world.
12. Zeus ordered Hephaestus, the god of sculptures, to make the most beautiful girl in the world.
13. Venus, the god of love, gave her the gift of beauty.
14. Hermes, the god of persuasion, gave her the powerful gift of the gab.
15. The god Apollo gave her the gift of music, she could play any instrument ever invented.
16. Pandora sat on the swing and sobbed, deeply regretting her curiosity.
17. The guests threw confetti whilst they cheered the happy couple before dancing.
18. The sun radiated bliss when the morning of the wedding day arrived making Pandora excited.
19. Pandora, scared, shivered before she ran inside.
20. Epimetheus soothed her by speaking calmly whilst holding her hand.

21. Hope fluttered past Pandora who looked up, faintly smiling.
22–31. The main character in the story is Pandora. She was sculpted by the god of sculptures to be the most beautiful girl in the world. She received many gifts from the gods, beauty, persuasion, music and a gold jar which she must never open. Prometheus warned his brother Epimetheus to be cautious of girls bearing gifts from the gods, but to no avail. Epimetheus proposed to Pandora who accepted.
32. both refer to gifts of the gods.
33. encourages an emotional response
34. relates to Pandora, the key character
35. It immediately creates sympathy for Pandora and encourages us to view the story from her point of view.
36. Pandora was all alone at the beginning of the story because she was sculpted rather than being brought up in a family.

| Expectations | Quotation |
|---|---|
| 37. Pandora would open the jar. | 38. 'The lid was tightly screwed down and the gods told her never ever to open it.' |
| 39. Pandora would cause trouble. | 40. 'If the gods have given her gifts, then beware.' |
| 41. Pandora would not be happy for very long. | 42. 'The moonlight reflected the gilded gold of the jar and dazzled Pandora. She was so happy…' |

| Conflict | Quotation |
|---|---|
| 43. Zeus was angry that fire had been given to human beings. | 44. 'Zeus was angry… because Prometheus, a Titan, had stolen his fire and given it to the mortals.' |
| 45. The brother's different view of Pandora. | 46. 'Epimetheus ignored his brother's warning.' |
| 47. Pandora and Prometheus are not friendly towards each other. | 48. 'Kissing Epimetheus, ignoring the dark looks of his brother Prometheus.' |

49. Pandora opens the jar
50. She is materialistic
51. The clouds obscured the moon and a low groan came from the bottom of the jar

| Cheerful mood | Sombre mood |
|---|---|
| 52. 'feasting, drinking and dancing' | 53. 'the dark looks of his brother Prometheus' |
| 54. 'The moonlight reflected the gilded gold of the jar and dazzled Pandora.' | 55. 'The clouds obscured the moon and a low groan came from the bottom of the jar.' |
| 56. 'when she smiles, the sun shines. When she laughs, the birds sing' | 57. 'She's nothing but trouble.' |

58. 'gift of the gab'
59. 'She was sure to be signed by a leading record label'
60. 'She had even sung her heart out to all the number ones and beat everyone on SongSuperStar.'
61. '…premier league, handsome husband who was really good at football.'
62. 'Or could there be designer jewellery…'
63. It makes the story easier to understand for children.
64. It suggests that Pandora is materialistic and ungrateful.
65. "Pandora sighed, fearing the winged thing's name was Ugly and all her good looks would instantly vanish."
66. third person
67. The repetition of 'every' emphasises the world wide impact of Pandora opening the jar.
68. Hope was put in the jar by a kind goddess who took pity on mankind.
69. The meaning Pandora is ironic because Pandora is not a gift but releases all the evils of the world.
70. The title has two meanings, it refers to the jar that Pandora is given but also to the cruel 'gift' that Zeus gives mankind.

## Paper 2

1. third
2. objective
3. Miss Blake
4. She is covering a lesson.
5. Maths
6. line 29
7. a tidy classroom
8. line 4
9. to show she is in charge / to make her feel important
10. yes

11. lines 19–23 → Miss Blake feels uncomfortable in this environment because the pupils know more about art than she does
12. lines 19 and 24 → The pupils settle down to their work quickly
13. lines 25–26 → The pupils do not need Miss Blake for anything
14. line 30 → Miss Blake thinks she is not very good at art
15. lines 5–8 → Miss Blake likes order, discipline and authority in her classroom
16. lines 9–10 → The pupils are confident in their art skills
17. lines 2–4 → The classroom is a stimulating environment
18. line 16 → There are different expectations of behaviour in the art class
19. line 32 → Miss Blake resented the pupils' creativity
20. line 28 → Miss Blake wanted to get involved in the art lesson
21. cover teacher
22. subject
23. tone
24. dismissive
25. strict
26. alliteration
27. sibilance
28. clusters of three
29. negative clusters of three
30. alliteration
31. internal rhyme
32. half rhyme / alliteration
33. half-rhyme
34. clusters of three
35. sibilance
36. jealous
37. uneven
38. perspective / opinion
39. vivid, light, dazzling
40. reveal, disclose
41. inspiration
42. creativity
43. colours
44. imagination
45. suspected
46. never
47. first
48. then
49. always
50. before
51. easily
52. 4
53. 2
54. 1
55. 3
56. kiln
57. collage
58. exhibition
59. frieze
60. perspective
61. acrylic
62. The pupils were asked by Miss Blake if they needed help.
63. The art lesson was finished early by Miss Blake.

64. With patience, drawing can be learnt by everyone.
65. A new art and design block is being built by the school.
66. This makes her name and her role important by separating them with punctuation.
67. The poet brackets 'Art' with commas to show that Miss Blake does not think very highly of it.
68. The use of a semi-colon suggests that the pupils are keen to get on with their lesson.
69. The lack of punctuation shows the creativity of the activities.
70. The lack of punctuation over so many lines suggests a build up of emotion for Miss Blake and ends with a sense of regret and jealousy.

## Paper 3
1. Act 1 Scene 2
2. There has been a shipwreck.
3. To give the impression that they have been shipwrecked.
4. To show clearly who is speaking.
5. Viola gives money to the Captain.
6. possibly / by chance
7. broken
8. friend
9. single man
10. gossip
11. To set the scene and tell the audience where the characters are.
12. The sailors and the Captain.
13. 'My brother, he is in Elysium'
14. They would either nod, shake their heads or look away.
15. Three hours travel from Illyria.
16. the Captain
17. Orsino
18. no
19. noble
20. A woman Orsino is in love with.
21. 'What country is this, friends?'
22. 'What do you sailors think?'
23. 'Here is money for saying that.'
24. 'And still is, or was until recently.'
25. 'Only a month ago, I went from here.'
26. courage
27. hope
28. He tied himself to the mast and kept his head above water.
29. 'Whereto thy speech serves for authority.'
30. A month ago.
31–40. In this scene, the audience is introduced to Viola who has landed on shore after being shipwrecked. Her third question, 'What think you, sailors?' tells the audience that even though she has been saved from the storm, she is upset at being separated from her brother who she believes is in Elysium which means she thinks he is dead / drowned. Shakespeare shows us that she is upset because she changes her mind quickly in the next line and says 'Perchance he is not drowned'. However, we know she is not certain about this because she asks the sailors what they think. The Captain's purpose in this scene is to reassure / convince Viola that her brother has survived the storm.

He does this first by reminding Viola that she has survived; 'It is perchance that you yourself were saved.' Shakespeare gives the Captain a variety of words to convince Viola such as; 'true', 'comfort' and 'assure'.
41. 'Orsino. I have heard my father name him.' → Put hands to heart
42. 'For saying so, there's gold.' → Get up and walk to the Captain and give him something
43. 'O my poor brother!- and so perchance may he be.' → Kneel and put hands together in prayer
44. 'What think you sailors?' → Run to each sailor and touch their arm or shoulder to answer the question
45. 'My brother, he is in Elysium.' → Put hands to face and sob silently
46. 'like Arion on the dolphin's back' → simile
47. 'Whereto thy speech serves for authority, The like of him. Know'st thou this country?' → end-rhyme
48. 'I saw him hold acquaintance with the waves' → personification
49. 'Assure yourself, after our ship did split' → sibilance
50. 'A noble duke, in nature / As in name.' → alliteration
51. true
52. true
53. true
54. true
55. false
56. false
57. false
58. true
59. false
60. true
61. applause
62. playwright
63. spotlight
64. improvise
65. costume
66. director
67. performance
68. rehearsal
69. entrance
70. theatre

## Paper 4
1. 1.2 billion
2. 25
3. 500 million
4. 1990
5. two million
6. four out of five
7. sub-Saharan Africa
8. 2015
9. nearly a third to less than a fifth
10. 2.6 billion
11. alpaca, line 31

12. trend, line 21
13. reform, line 24
14. sustained, line 21
15. absolute, line 50
16. vulnerable, line 77
17. eradicate, title
18. asset, line 71
19. proportion, line 14
20. relative, line 48
21. Example 1: food
    Evidence: "people will have at least the minimum necessary to feed... themselves."
22. Example 2: clothes
    Evidence: "people will have at least the minimum necessary to…clothe themselves."
23. Example 3: heating
    Evidence: "They live in small shacks with no heating…"
    (other answers could include; clean water, sanitation, electricity)
24. The article describes extreme poverty as people who live on less than $1 or 50p per day.
25. South Asia
26. The MDG targets might not be reached if poverty continues to increase in sub-Saharan Africa. OR The impact of climate change will be an obstacle for the achievement of the MDG.
27. sub-Saharan Africa
28. The international community
29. As the standard of living has risen for many people, it is unfair that so many people should be living in extreme poverty.
30. Reform international trade and tackle climate change.
31. Reforming international trade would mean that developing countries like those in sub-Saharan Africa would 'receive fair prices for their goods' whilst slowing down climate change would reduce the chance of natural disasters resulting in 'floods, droughts and food shortages.'
32. The MDG is not aiming to completely eradicate poverty because there are so many people who live in extreme poverty; they are seen as the highest priority.
33. Most alpaca farmers in Macusani have scarcely enough to eat and live in tiny hovels without any heating.
34. relative poverty
35. The article defines absolute poverty as living on $1 per day whereas the average earnings for alpaca farmers are less than $2 per day.
36. The greatest concern for the alpaca farmers is the fact that the glacier is melting due to climate change, which could mean that they have no source of water.
37. The impact of the lack of water supply will mean that the community will have to move somewhere else and give up their livelihood.
38. *Example answer*: I think that this must worry the children a great deal making it difficult for them to concentrate.
39. Everyone in the world who contributes negatively to climate change would be responsible for the glacier melting

40. Rich countries could make changes to international trade and halt climate change to support poor countries.
41. The article includes the account of Lucas Riquelme to make the reader realise the impact of poverty on the individual.
42. The two factors responsible for the food shortages in Ethiopia in 2008 are drought and rising prices.
43. The DFID programme asked people to work to improve the facilities in the community and gave them food and money in exchange.
44. The DFID did not help all the vulnerable people because it had to concentrate on the most vulnerable people.
45. Aster Kumar works for the DFID project on soil conservation and tree planting projects five days a week.
46. This is not voluntary because she receives food and payment whilst her work on the farmlands will support her in the future.
47. The programme supports people like Aster Kurma in the short term by providing them with food and money.
48. The programme supports people like Aster Kurma in the long term by providing them with facilities to support themselves.
49. Aster Kumar would not be able to feed her family if the programme did not exist.
50. The article includes the account of Aster Kurma to encourage the reader to think about the problems of poverty in a personalised way.
51–65. Example Answers: Make sure that the answers include the points referred to in the question.

| | Key Point | Evidence | Explanation |
|---|---|---|---|
| Introduction | "2.6 billion people live on less than £1.00 a day." | Don't you think that the figure is remarkable considering we live in the 21st century? | As my local Member of Parliament, I would like you to look at ways of making sure that everyone gets a fair price for their products. |
| Paragraph 1 | "Much could be achieved by reforming international trade" | Don't you think it is unfair that poor people receive poor prices for their food which will only prevent them from escaping the poverty trap? | I know that changing a small thing can make a huge difference and so I have asked for a bike for Christmas so I can cycle to school instead of my father taking me every day in the car. |
| Paragraph 2 | "Halting climate change will also be essential" | If I can make a positive step to reduce climate change, what positive changes could someone as powerful as a Member of Parliament do? | At school and at home we are always encouraged to eat healthily but many children do not even have enough to eat, never mind eat healthily. |

| | | | |
|---|---|---|---|
| Paragraph 3 | "850 million people go to bed hungry every day." | I cannot imagine what it must be like to experience that level of poverty but writing to ask you to support the Millennium Development Goal could reduce that figure. | I realise that I am only a pupil at a school but even I can see that many things in this world are unjust. |
| Conclusion | "In a world in which many people are better off than ever before, it is unacceptable that so many others should be struggling to survive." | One day, I will be able to vote for people that will be able to make a difference; you can make that difference today by supporting the Millennium Development Goal. | In Britain, we are fortunate to be able to vote. Let us all use it to make a difference to those less fortunate than ourselves! |

66. I would use formal language because the letter is to a Member of Parliament.
67. I would use rhetorical questions to encourage the reader to agree with the point that has been made.
68. I would use personal pronouns to engage the reader and persuade them to listen to my argument.
69. I would use statistics because they make my points more valid.
70. I would use a personalised account because it would encourage the reader to empathise with my point of view.

**Paper 5**
1. unprecedented, line 7
2. diminished, line 27
3. empathy, line 23
4. malleable, line 39
5. predisposing, line 21
6. entities, line 35
7. stymie, line 25
8. scaremongering, line 71
9. perpetual, line 33
10. benign, line 45
    *Suggested answers, check the sense within the sentence*
11. hasty
12. definite
13. long-term
14. scandalous
15. intolerances / biases
16. delicately
17. ignore the
18. carelessness
19. distinct
20. worries / fears
21. Children who use technology frequently expect very quick responses which may result in a shorter attention span.
22. "Perhaps when, back in the real word, such responses are not forthcoming, attention deficit hyperactivity disorder will result."
23. Using computers and video games frequently means that children live for the moment in a world that is not real.
24. "This is a literal world where everything is not related to previous experiences or any wider context."

25. Children's actions during a video game do not have real life consequences which mean that they take more risks.

26. "If most of a young child's actions take place on screen and so have no permanent consequences it will prove a bad lesson when it comes to real life."

27. Children who play video games frequently are not communicating with real people so they will not develop the ability to empathise with others.

28. "Interacting in person with others… (is a) good way of learning about how others feel and think."

29. Playing video games frequently over a long period of time may prevent children from understanding abstract ideas or sophisticated imagery because the games are so literal.

30. "Might constant exposure to a literal world mean that the brain remains infant-like?"

31. Constant playing of video games can mean that we do not develop as individuals.

32. "If we live perpetually in the moment, …might our sense of self be in jeopardy?"

33. The combination of a short-attention span, lack of empathy and underdeveloped self-identity are features of a wide range of mental health conditions.

34. "…the mindset profiled above is similar to that seen in a…range of conditions such as compulsive gambling and schizophrenia, and has been linked to an underactive prefrontal cortex."

35. Just because someone does not like using the internet or video games, this does not mean that they are damaging to children.

36. "…scientific evidence does not support my personal prejudices."

37. There is no scientific evidence to suggest that video games damage the brain.

38. " …they are reviews of the many existing studies that help us understand whether screen culture is genuinely damaging the mind and brain."

39. Scientific research has shown that playing video games improves reaction time.

40. "…video gamers had quicker reactions than non-gamers, and that this edge was not achieved at the expense of being impulsive or making more mistakes."

41. Scientific research has shown that playing video games has a positive benefit of increasing the speed the brain works.

42. "In other words gamers' brains worked faster, with no loss of accuracy,…"

43. Using the internet does not have a significant effect on people's happiness.

44. "…the National Changhua University of Education in Taiwan, found that internet use was linked to a slight reduction in people's sense of well-being, but one so slender as to be irrelevant."

45. Young people's use of social networking sites is a method to improve their social life rather than being detrimental to the ability to socialise.

46. "…, research on young people shows that use of the sites is associated with a better social life in the real world because they use the services to enhance their existing relationships…"

47. It is understandable to be worried about the rapid advancements of technology but it is important to be balanced when assessing the potential risks and benefits.

48. "…personal opinion is no substitute for hard evidence, and as scientists we do the public a disservice if we confuse the two."

49. The article includes the job titles because it gives credibility to their arguments.

50. She suggests that the brain is very responsive to the surrounding environment.

51. As the environment around us changes, our brain evolves to adapt.

52. Baroness Greenfield thinks that living in the moment means that we do not appreciate the impact our actions may have on others or ourselves.

53. She suggests that living in the moment teaches children that their actions do not have consequences in the real world, which is false.

54. Baroness Greenfield suggests that we are losing the capacity to understand others because young people do not interact socially but spend a long time playing video games and using the internet.

55. She suggests that Twitter demonstrates that we do not like to be isolated from others and need to have feedback from the people around us.

56. *(Select five)* The features of the mindset profile described by Baroness Greenfield are; short attention span, reliance on adrenalin buzz, inaccuracy, recklessness, reduced ability to empathise, lack of understanding of abstract ideas and metaphors and a poor understanding of the self.

57. She suggests that the mindset profile is similar to a compulsive gambler, or someone suffering from schizophrenia.

58. *Example answer:* My suggestion is that spending a long time in front of a video game or on the internet could result in the brain failing to develop which would result in a permanent childlike state.

59. Vaughan Bell states that the evidence does not show that screen culture is damaging our brains or our ability to think.

60. He claims that internet use is nothing to worry about because it is simply new technology and compares it to the telephone which must have caused people to be anxious when it was invented.

61. He claims that the media exaggerates their stories to make headlines rather than base them in fact.

62. He states that scientists must never use their personal beliefs to affect the way they carry out research or present their findings.

63–70. *Example answer: Make sure that the answers include the points referred to in the question.*

The contrasting points of view come from respected and educated people; a neuropsychologist, Vaughan Bell and a neuroscientist, Baroness Greenfield. Whilst both are credible, Greenfield refers vaguely to scientific studies whereas Bell actually references when and where the studies have been completed. This provides Bell with more credibility than Greenfield. Greenfield's argument is not as persuasive as Bell's because she uses more modal auxiliaries such as "perhaps", "might" and "if" which suggests that there is no concrete evidence to support her argument. Although her argument is well constructed through the use of linking adverbs such as "first", "second" and "third" to help the reader follow her points, the language is too scientific. Bell offers evidence from scientific articles that have summarised years of research, which means that his viewpoint is more persuasive. Additionally, Bell's argument is easier to follow because he uses less formal scientific language than Greenfield and some readers will be confused by her use of scientific terminology like "underactive prefrontal cortex". I found that Bell's article was more persuasive because it was less formal, clearer and made references to hard evidence. If video games and the internet are used responsibly and in moderation, they can make huge benefits to our lives. Like anything, if we use them without consideration for the well-being of others and ultimately ourselves, they have the potential to be damaging. Personally, I think that we should not be afraid of new technology but like everything in life, it has advantages and disadvantages.

**Paper 6**

1. endeavour
2. convulsive
3. infinite
4. lustrous
5. livid
6. extinguish
7. toil
8. aspect
9. agitate
10. infuse
11. ardour
12. traversing
13. proportion
14. compose
15. catastrophe
16. delineate
17. demoniacal
18. hue
19. lassitude
20. tumult
21. incomplete
22. nationalism

23. autobiography
24. micrometer
25. disloyal
26. brotherhood
27. friendship
28. lioness
29. Londoner
30. romanticism

*Suggested Answers*

31. It was on a dreary night in November that I saw the achievement of my work.
32. It was already one in the morning; the rain pattered dismally against the panes, and I had no electricity.
33. How can I describe my emotions at this catastrophe, or how can I describe the monster that I had carefully and painstakingly tried to create?
34. Because of this, I had deprived myself of rest and health.
35. At long last, tiredness won, and I threw myself on the bed in my clothes, trying to seek a few moments of forgetfulness.

| | | |
|---|---|---|
| 36. | Frankenstein ran away from the creature to his bedroom and tried to settle his mind to sleep. | 5 |
| 37. | Frankenstein was bitterly disappointed by his experiment and sickened by the creature. | 6 |
| 38. | Frankenstein had a nightmare that Elizabeth turned into the buried body of his dead mother. | 8 |
| 39. | One night in November, Frankenstein nervously arranged his medical instruments. | 1 |
| 40. | The creature came into Frankenstein's bedroom and held out his arm to Frankenstein. | 9 |
| 41. | Around one in the morning, the creature opened his eyes and his body shook. | 3 |
| 42. | Frankenstein ran away from the monster and walked up and down for the rest of the night. | 10 |
| 43. | Frankenstein had worked for two years on his greatest ambition which was to create life. | 2 |
| 44. | The creature's appearance was horrifying to Frankenstein. | 4 |
| 45. | Frankenstein dreamt of kissing Elizabeth's lips which turned them to the colour of death. | 7 |

46. Shelley uses a first person point of view in this chapter to encourage us to see the creature through Frankenstein's eyes.
47. Lines 7–8
48. 'I had worked hard for nearly two years, for the sole purpose of infusing life into an inanimate body.'
49. 'For this I had deprived myself of rest and health'
50. 'and breathless horror and disgust filled my heart.'
51. 'demoniacal corpse to which I had so miserably given life.'
52. 'His jaws opened, and he muttered some inarticulate sounds, while a grin wrinkled his cheeks. He might have spoken, but I did not hear; one hand was stretched out,'
53. true
54. true
55. false
56. true

57. false
58. true
59. true
60. false
61. images of death
62. contrasting imagery
63. pathetic fallacy
64. images of death
65. contrasting imagery
66. images of death
67. positive imagery
68. metaphor
69. pathetic fallacy
70. images of death

**Paper 7**

1. taught
2. implore
3. outlandish
4. absolute
5. sovereign
6. immoral
7. entreaty
8. lecture
9. intimidate
10. conceited
11. You listen to your king/lord too; both have spoken.
12. I think you speak like a boy.
13. As king of the desert you would shine.
14. If you are a woman, yes. My thought is for you.
15. O rascal, would you battle with your king/lord?
16. And you, me and the gods below.
17. Has it come to this to threaten me?
18. Living, the maid shall never be your bride.
19. Vain fool to instruct your betters; you will regret it.
20. When you speak, must no man reply?
21. Haemon is Creon's son.
22. Line 5: "HAEMON: I beg for justice, father, nothing more." and line 32 "HAEMON: Were you not my father, I had said thou err'st."
23. Haemon's plea for justice
24. Haemon wants Creon to let Antigone live.
25. The Chorus advises Creon to listen to Haemon.
26. Creon says this because he is angry that Haemon who is his subject and son is giving him, the King and his father, advice.
27. The Chorus is closer in age to Creon.
28. Creon says "What, would you have us at our age be schooled," which suggests that he is including the Chorus.
29. The Chorus offers advice and commentary for Creon.
30. Line 1: "CHORUS: If he says anything appropriate, listen to him, King."
31. Creon
32. Haemon
33. This is an example of a rhetorical question.
34. Haemon's answer is that if you only rule for yourself, then you are not really ruling anything.
35. This shows the Creon rules for himself rather than for his people.

36. The King would make a good ruler in a desert where there are no other people.
37. Desert and shine.
38. They are connected by the image of heat.

In any order:
39. Justice spoken by Haemon
40. Rule spoken by Creon
41. State spoken by Creon (and Haemon)
42. Monarch spoken by Creon

In any order:
43. beardless boy
44. O rascal
45. Vain fool
46. Play not the spaniel
47. a woman's slave
48. Three of the following or something similar: just, fair, wise, brave, committed, steady.
49. Line 20 "HAEMON: Because I see thee wrongfully wicked."
50. Death
51. Line 27 "CREON: Living, the maid shall never be thy bride."
52. Haemon will see Antigone die.
53. Line 37–38 "Off with the hateful thing that she may die At once, beside her bridegroom, in his sight."
54. The structure changes to show the climax of the scene.
55. The dramatist has given Haemon the last four lines as they are the most powerful and set up the ending of the play.
56. The Chorus' opening comments suggest Haemon and Creon are in conflict.
57. They ask both Creon and Haemon to "listen" to each other and comment that they have "both spoken well".
58. This informs the audience that Creon and Haemon have spoken before on the matter but have not listened to each other's point of view.
59. The key theme introduced is how to rule a state.
60. Haemon comments that "A State for one man is no State at all."
61. This suggests that Creon has not listened to his people and only rules for himself.
62. Haemon's argument becomes emotive because he states that he will die with Antigone.
63. "So she shall die, but I will die with her."
64. This shows the audience how strongly he feels about Antigone.
65. Sophocles turns the audience against Creon because he does not try to convince his son not to kill himself with Antigone but is more angry about the fact that Haemon has questioned his authority.
66. "By heaven, thou shalt not rate/ And jeer and flout me without regard."
67. This shows that Creon's main concern is Haemon questioning his authority and that he cannot do this without paying the consequences.
68. Sophocles creates sympathy for Haemon and his point of view because he is willing to kill himself before he sees Antigone die.

69. "Think not that in my sight the maid shall die, / Or by my side".

70. This shows that he is prepared to sacrifice himself for Antigone.

**Paper 8**

1. First person
   *Example answer*

2–4. The first person narrative viewpoint is effective because it is more personalised and encourages the reader to feel sympathy directly with the speaker. The statement that opens the poem, 'Remember me' is almost a command and is directed towards the reader.

5. The persona is going to die.

6. The time of death is not revealed but she knows that it will happen and expects to die before her lover.

7. She asks her lover to remember her.

8. Remember her when she is gone

9. Remember her when he can no longer hold her hand

10. Remember her when she wanted to stay

11. Remember her when they cannot plan their future together

12. The semi-colon suggests a change in tone and in meaning.

13. It will be too late for her lover because she will be dead.

14. The tone changes in line 9.

15. The tone changes to show that the persona realises that her lover will not always remember her.

16. The two conflicting emotions Rossetti presents are love and sadness.
    *Example answer*

17–20. Rossetti refers to death indirectly throughout the poem using imagery such as 'silent land;' which suggests that she must speak now because at some point, she will not be able to communicate her feelings. The metaphor is effective because there is nowhere on earth that is truly silent and therefore this place must suggest death.
    *Example answer*

21–24. Rossetti describes how strong her love is in the present through imagining the moments of loss in the future. The repetition of 'when' in the first five lines indicates the sadness of the future moments that Rossetti is imagining her lover will experience when she is gone. This is further reinforced by the lines 'when no more day by day / You tell me of our future that you plann'd' suggesting that sadness is inevitable.

25. Barrett-Browning uses the first person viewpoint throughout the poem.

26. The first person viewpoint is effective because it is personal which suits the subject of the poem, which is love.

27. More than the anyone can experience in the universe (depth, breadth and height / My soul can reach).

28. When she is feeling low, her love inspires her to feel spiritual and virtuous ('when feeling out of sight / For the ends of Being and ideal Grace').

29. She loves him continuously throughout the ordinary events of the day ('I love thee to the level of everyday's/ Most quiet need').

30. She loves him every moment of her existence, day and night ('by sun and candle-light')

31. She loves him without reservation ('I love thee freely').

32. She loves with the passion that men have who fight for justice ('as men strive for Right').

33. She loves him with an innocent love ('I love thee purely').

34. She loves him as intensely as she loved the people she has lost and with the belief in love she had as a child ('I love thee with the passion put to use / In my old grief, and with my childhood's faith.').

35. The rhyme scheme in the poem is abba abba cdcdcd.

36. The form of the poem is a sonnet.

37. This form of poem is appropriate because a sonnet is usually about love.

38. The pattern of rhythm in the poem is iambic pentameter.

39. The iambic pentameter is appropriate because it is the form of rhythm that most closely resembles direct speech.

40. The tone of the poem is joyful and jubilant which is expressed by the line 'I love thee with the breath, smiles, tears, of all my life!' demonstrating the exuberance the persona feels.

41. Barrett-Browning gives the theme of love more emphasis in her sonnet.
    *Example answer*

42–45. In the poem, Barrett-Browning presents love as the very reason for her existence. The repetition of the numerous ways that she loves her partner begins with 'depth and breadth and height / My soul can reach', an intensity which is emphasised by the unnecessary repetition of 'and' in the line. The simple repetition of 'I love thee' which occurs nine times in only fourteen lines highlights the extent of her feelings for her partner.
    *Example answer*

46. Both poems present love and death but in differing ways.

47. 'gone away' and 'I shall but love thee better after death'.

48. Whereas Barrett-Browning waits until the very last line to mention death, Rossetti's reference to death occurs in the first line.

49. The way the poets choose to structure the themes of love and death reveals that Rossetti's poem is more about the inevitable fading of love after death whereas Barrett-Browning's poem is more about the celebration of love in spite of death.

50. Rossetti's poem does not refer directly to death or love in her poem whereas Barrett-Browning explicitly mentions love and death.

51. 'How do I love thee?' and 'Remember me when I am gone away,'

52. In Barrett-Browning's poem, the love immediately referred to in the opening line is further emphasised nine times throughout the poem whereas Rossetti's poem love is referred to as something that can only be remembered rather than directly experienced.

53. The explicit references to love in Barrett-Browning's poem compared to the indirect references to a remembered love in Rossetti's poem could suggest that Barrett-Browning is more confident that her love is eternal whereas Rossetti is sad because she knows it cannot last forever.

54. Although the content of the poems are different in the emphasis they give to love and death, both poems are in sonnet form.

55. The poets change the tone of their poem at line six of the sonnets.

56. Rossetti's poem changes from a request to her lover to remember her to an acceptance that he may forget. However, Barrett-Browning's poem changes from metaphorical representations of love to directly stating how much she loves her partner.

57. The shift in emphasis is the same in each poem but Rossetti's takes on a sadder tone whereas Barrett-Browning's poem takes on more joyful tone.

58. Rossetti's sonnet uses less positive imagery than Barrett-Browning's sonnet.

59. 'For if the darkness and corruption leave / A vestige of the thoughts that once I had' and 'For the ends of Being and ideal Grace'

60. Although each poet refers to death, they do it in contrasting ways.

61. Rossetti's sombre metaphor for death as 'darkness and corruption' contrasts with Barrett-Browning's more hopeful imagery of death 'ends of Being and ideal Grace' because it suggests a more spiritual and elevated death.

62. The object of love in both poems is also different.

63. 'How do I love thee?' and 'Remember me'

64. In Barrett-Browning's poem the persona talks about how much love she has for her partner whereas in Rossetti's poem the persona requests her partner to remember her rather than stating how much she loves him.

65. The use of personal pronouns in the poems indicate that Rossetti's poem is more about how she will not be remembered although she wants to be whereas Barrett-Browning's poem is concentrated on how much the persona loves the object of her affections.

66. The differences in the way the poets describe love and death are evident in what they emphasise, the tone and the imagery they use.

67. Remember

68. 'Love' is referenced ten times in Barrett-Browning's poem whereas 'Remember' is mentioned five times.

69. It could be that the each poet is describing a different time in their relationships; the way Rossetti asks her partner to remember her, suggests that they have been together for a while whereas Barrett-Browning's poem suggests that she is celebrating the beginning of a relationship.

70. I think both poems are powerful expressions of feelings; Rossetti's is more realistic whereas Barrett-Browning's is more idealistic.

## Paper 9

1. enlist, line 3
2. consume, line 17
3. irreverent, line 41
4. slumped, line 8
5. dysfunctional, line 6
6. implicitly, line 43
7. breach, line 36
8. regulator, line 36
9. endorse, line 43
10. acknowledge, line 30
11. The Department of Health is campaigning for the nation to follow a healthy lifestyle.
12. They are campaigning for this because one in five children will be overweight or obese by next year, obesity costs the National Health Service £4.2 billion a year at the moment, and these costs will double by 2050.
13. Healthy eating and an increase in physical activity.
14. They hope people will see themselves when watching The Simpsons.
15. Bart Simpson
16. He probably achieves the government recommended hour of exercise a day.
17. Lisa Simpson
18. She is a vegetarian and likely to eat the recommended 5 portions of fruit or vegetables a day.
19. Homer Simpson and Bart Simpson.
20. It is suggested that it will be effective because they are imperfect, so people will be more likely to listen to them.

41–47. In any order:

| Point | Evidence (line reference) | Explanation |
|---|---|---|
| Eat together | 18 | Suggests regular and shared mealtimes |
| Care about each other | 18 | Suggests a supportive family |
| Share difficulties | 19 | Suggests that they help each other get through difficult times |
| Bart is physically very active | 16 | Encourages children to be active in a fun way |
| Lisa is a vegetarian | 17 | Encourages children to eat healthy food |
| Public are likely to take advice if characters are not | 44–47 | Suggests that improving your lifestyle is easy to do |

| Healthy living should be associated with something fun | 41 | Encourages people to keep to a healthy lifestyle |
|---|---|---|
| Popular | 28 | This means that more people will see the healthy eating campaign |
| Similar to real-life families | 28 | This will encourage families to take up good habits |

48. Homer Simpson is well known for drinking beer and eating doughnuts which makes the decision to sponsor The Simpsons surprising.
49. The Department of Health has chosen to sponsor The Simpsons because they can reach a lot of people.
50. Some people have been critical of the decision because there are better examples of cartoon characters who support healthy eating.
51. Ofcom said that Domino's Pizza encouraged children to eat junk food. *Example answers*
52. "carrots, apples and pears."
53. "Supporting The Simpsons: Sometimes"
54. "…are a caring and sharing family, despite their many troubles."
55. "It is not what is said but who says it that matters."
56. The Minister for Public Health comments that The Simpsons are a family favourite setting an excellent example of how a family supports each other through difficult times.
57. For
58. The comment highlights the simple effectiveness of the method of communicating the message.
59. The Department of Health has chosen The Simpsons because people will be able to compare themselves with the family which will encourage them to make positive changes to their lifestyle.
60. For
61. This suggests that the Department of Health has thought carefully about how to encourage people to change their behaviour rather than tell them off.
62. Professor Gerard Hastings believes that if people hear a message from someone who is not perfect, they are more likely to listen.
63. For
64. This comment has credibility because it comes from someone who has studied how society behaves and responds to marketing messages. *Example answer*
65–70. I strongly agree with the Department of Health's decision to sponsor The Simpsons to encourage people to have a healthier lifestyle. Can you imagine the amazing things that we could spend £4.2 billion on? That is how much the National Health Service has to spend to treat obese people every year. If people took greater care of their health, ate more fruit and vegetables and exercised regularly, then we could spend the money on education, on outdoor and indoor facilities for children after school, or give every child in the country a free bicycle! Critics may say that Homer Simpson is better known for drinking beer and eating doughnuts but if he can change then so can other families.

## Paper 10

1. quadriceps
2. hamstring
3. gymnastic
4. tournament
5. triceps
6. qualify
7. mobility
8. medicine
9. athletic
10. agility
11. Wonderful or amazing or exceptional
12. Impressive or esteemed
13. To admit something as correct
14. Accepted
15. A position socially or professionally
16. Standing / position / rank
17. A remarkable person or occurrence
18. Marvel / wonder / miracle
19. To consider or regard
20. Supposed
21. Celebrate with cheering or clapping
22. Applause
23. To get back again
24. Recovered
25. To reject
26. Abstained from or avoided
27. To make something misshapen
28. bending
29. to carry out something with self-confidence
30. ease
31. This suggests that people closest to him knew him more like an ordinary close friend than a distant superhero.
32. It is surprising because he was only a small man and did not weigh very much.
33. It suggests that it was a commonly held belief.
34. The facts such as he was only 5ft 5in tall, weighed around 10st and yet was able to lift 475lb with his teeth, 635lb with one finger and 1,5000lb in a hand-and-thigh lift, and 3,200lb on his back support the students' assertions that he was 'one of the strongest men who ever lived.'
35. The article suggests that Joe Rollino's most impressive achievement was being awarded three Purple Hearts, a Silver Star and a Bronze star for his actions during the Second World War.
36. He was motivated to box when he saw a smaller man, Jack Dempsey, knock out a giant man when he was only 14.

37. As Joe Rollino was only a small man, he might have been a small teenager and therefore impressed at the courage that Dempsey showed during his fight.

38–39. He makes a comment 'You could sell me for scrap' which suggests that although he was permanently injured in the war, he could still make a joke about it.

40. Joe Rollino said he was born strong and therefore was always interested in his physical appearance.

41. 'Often known as the Great or Mighty Joe Rollino, or when in the boxing ring as Kid Dundee, and when in his home quarter familiarly nicknamed Puggy'

42. The repetition of three gives the impression that he was best known as a legendary or familiar figure rather than by his first and second name.

43. 'He abjured meat, cigarettes and alcohol,'

44. The repetition of three gives the impression that he avoided anything that would be bad for his health.

45. '…he was awarded three Purple Hearts, a Silver Star and a Bronze star…'

46. This repetition of three emphasises his courageous acts during the Second World War.

47. '…throwing combinations with aplomb, parrying and dipping like a 25-year-old.'

48. The repetition of three represents the flurry of movement of Joe Rollino's boxing style.

49. 'Though relatively small in stature he was confidently billed in the 1920s as "The World's Strongest Man".'

50. The opposing idea of being physically small and the world's strongest man creates a powerful impression of Joe Rollino's physical achievement.

51. 'Joe Rollino achieved something of the status of a superhero in New York'.

52. The repetition of the 's' reinforces the impact of the word superhero.

53. 'Even in such prodigious company it was conceded that Rollino, who still worked out regularly in the gym, was "in pretty good shape", **though** "he walked a little slow".'

54. The concession subordinating conjunction 'though' indicates the reality of the impact of Joe Rollino's age as it comes before the statement that he walked slowly.

55–56. The article does not open with biographical details such as Joe Rollino's age or background to ensure that his 'status of a superhero' is given the most importance. The word superhero encourages the reader to expect the information that follows to provide examples of his superhero status.

57. Joe Rollino apologised for deforming a quarter because he used to be able to bend a dime.

58. The writer breaks up the sentence with a quotation from Joe to reduce the seriousness of his injury.

59. The writer links the sentences through the idea of bravery; first listing the medals before highlighting his injury and his humorous attitude towards it.

60. Although the whole article proclaims Joe Rollino's physical prowess, the article suggests that he met his death because he could not walk fast enough.

61–70. *Example Answer (make sure the answer includes all points listed in the question)*

The writer immediately creates the impression that Joe Rollino was a legend through the use of alliteration and powerful imagery in the first sentence. By opening with 'something of the status of a superhero' the reader is encouraged to view the text that follows with this in mind. The writer uses dramatic adjectives such as 'strongest', 'Mighty' and 'Great' to reinforce the view of Rollino as a legendary figure. This view is emphasised through the adverbs the writer chooses, such as the fact that even though he was over a hundred years old, he 'still worked out regularly in the gym'. The article concludes with a repetition of three; strongman, weightlifter and boxer, emphasising Joe Rollino's physical magnificence that the article starts with. The writer continues to use the past tense throughout the article until 'It is thought', three quarters through the article; as such we realise that the article is an obituary. I think it is an astonishing account of Joe Rollino's life; extremely compelling and rather sad as he did not die of natural causes.

**Acknowledgements**

**p24.** text reproduced by kind permission of The Times (nisyndication.com)

**p44.** text reproduced by kind permission of Methuen Drama, an imprint of A&C Black Publishers Ltd. Permission for rehearsals/performances and/or recordings of any sort whatsoever to be addressed to Micheline Steinberg Associates, 104 Great Portland Street, London W1W 6PE (info@steinplays.c

**p58.** text reproduced by kind permission The Times (nisyndication.com)

**p64.** text reproduced by kind permission The Times (nisyndication.com)